Contents

Chapter IV Nigeria's Young Voices and Dreams

Abbreviations and symbols

adj	adjective		
f./ff.	and the following page(s)/line(s)		
fml	formal		
infml	informal		
jdn., jdm.	*jemanden, jemandem*		
l., ll.	line, lines		
n	noun		
p., pp.	page, pages		
pl	plural		
sb.	somebody		
sl	slang		
sth.	something		
v	verb		

cornelsen.de
Code: pigene

The webcode can be entered at *www.cornelsen.de* to connect you directly to a website with additional material.

⊙

Audio/video on CD extra contained in the Teacher's Manual (978-3-06-035909-7)

Approaching the Giant of Africa

Part A
Basics

A1 Getting started

1 What do you know about Nigeria? What do you associate with the country? Note down words or phrases which come to mind.
2 Study the pictures on this page.
  a Make notes on the following questions (→ Language help):
  – What aspects of Nigeria are depicted in the pictures?
  – What do the pictures tell you about the country, its culture and everyday life?
  b Speaking In groups of three, share your first impressions and discuss whether the pictures support, extend or contradict your view on Nigeria (→ Language help).

A

B

C

> **Language help**
> depict sth. · symbolize sth. · represent sth. · relate to sth. · support the idea of sth. · underline the impression of sth.

A2 Nigeria – facts and figures

Work with a partner. **Partner A:** work on task **1** below.
Partner B: go to p. 75.

1 Guess the relevant figures for **Nigeria** and fill them in the table below. The figures for Germany may help you as a reference.

	Nigeria	Germany	South Africa
Life expectancy	_____ years	80.9 years	_____ years
Median age	_____ years	47.4 years	_____ years
Access to improved drinking water supply	_____ %	100 %	_____ %
Access to improved sanitation facilities	_____ %	99.2 %	_____ %
Access to electricity	_____ %	100 %	_____ %
Internet users	_____ %	89.6 %	_____ %
GDP by sector Agriculture	_____ %	0.7 %	_____ %
Industry	_____ %	30.7 %	_____ %
Services	_____ %	68.6 %	_____ %

Statistics from: www.cia.gov, 2019

Annotations
– median age: the age from which point half of the population is younger and the other half is older
– GDP = gross domestic product: *Bruttoinlandsprodukt*

2 **Speaking** Present your findings to your partner and ask him/her for the correct figures. Correct your table if necessary. Discuss which facts surprised you most (→ Language help).

Language help
have a life expectancy of … · have access to … · be provided with … · account for … % of the GDP

3 Speaking Your partner will tell you some other facts about **Nigeria**.
If necessary, provide him/her with the right figures from the table
below. Discuss which facts surprised you most.

	Nigeria	Germany	South Africa
Religions*	51.6% Muslim 46.9% Christian 1.54% others 0% none	55.3% Christian 5% Muslim 2.7% others 37% none	_____ % Muslim _____ % Christian _____ % traditional African _____ % others _____ % none
Land area	923,768 km²	357,022 km²	_____ km²
Population	203,452,505 (rank 7 in the world)	80,457,737 (rank 19 in the world)	_____ (rank _____ in the world)
Population below poverty line	70%	16.7%	_____ %
Urban population	50.3	77.3	_____
Literacy rate	59.6%	99%	_____ %
Unemployment rate	16.5%	3.8%	_____ %

The percentages here are rounded; hence they can add up to more/less than 100%.
Statistics from: www.cia.gov, 2019

Language help
be affiliated with a religion · cover an area of … ·
the fourth most populous country in the world … · amount to sth.

4 a With your partner, choose **five aspects** you are interested in and research the facts for **South Africa**. Enter them in the tables on pp. 6 and 7.

   b `Speaking` Get together with another team. Present and discuss your findings (→ Language help).

Language help

in comparison to … · in contrast to … · on the one hand …, on the other hand … · whereas … · considering … it can be said that … · the statistics underline the fact that …

A3 Nigeria's geographical challenges

Nigeria is a country with an extremely diverse geography.
This brings some challenges with it.

Comprehension

1 `Viewing` Watch the video on Nigeria's geographical challenges (→ Annotations).

Video online:
▯ ⊙ cornelsen.de
+ ◁) Code: pigene

   a Look at the diagram below: which resources (**1**–**4**) can be found in which of the two Nigerian regions (**A**, **B**)? Write the appropriate letter(s) in the spaces provided next to the resources on the right.

1 natural gas: _____

A northern half

2 rubber: _____

B highlands in the south

3 oil palms: _____

4 dairy products: _____

Annotations
– dairy: made from milk
– Igbo (also 'Ibo') ['iːbəʊ]: person belonging to the Igbo people, an ethnic group living predominantly in the southeast of Nigeria

   b Tick the challenges faced by Nigeria that are mentioned in the video.

      A There isn't enough land for agriculture in Nigeria.
      B The Igbo have had too much political influence.
      C There is competition over natural resources between Nigeria's regions.
      D Nigeria is an ethnically divided country.
      E Nigeria isn't managing the money made from oil in a clever way.
      F Its population will have grown to 390 million by 2025.

2 `Writing` Outline Nigeria's diversity as presented in the video and point out why this leads to challenges and struggles within the state.

> **Language help**
> form a boundary between … · be located in/on … · be divided along … · produce cash crops · support Nigeria's population · location of natural resources · abundant reserves of sth. · be home to sb./sth. · geographical distribution of (ethnic groups) · projected population · Nigeria's countryside · urbanization · dominant ethnic group · settle its division · exert influence over sb./sth. · face challenges

A4 'This is Nigeria!'

In May 2018, German Federal Foreign Office State Minister Michelle Müntefering visited Nigeria for the first time.

1 `Mediation` You are writing for an international internet forum on travelling in Africa. Based on the text below, write a blog entry in English in which you point out what might make Nigeria attractive but also dangerous for travellers.

Es stimmt, was man mir geraten hat: Vor der ersten Reise erst einmal alles zu vergessen, was man über Afrika zu wissen meint. Nigeria präsentiert sich als Land der Chancen und Potentiale. Gleichzeitig gibt es Risiken und Unwägbarkeiten in dem größten afrikanischen Land mit
5 seinen rund 190 Millionen Einwohnern, davon allein rund 12 Millionen in der Metropole Lagos, in der die Aufbruchstimmung einer jungen, selbstbewussten Generation Nigerianerinnen und Nigerianer spürbar ist und die in einer quirligen start-up-Landschaft und boomenden Kreativwirtschaft in „Nollywood" zum Ausdruck kommt. Künstlerinnen und
10 Künstler und eine aktive Zivilgesellschaft mit starken engagierten Frauen zeichnen Nigeria als ein Land der Chancen und der kulturellen Vielfalt aus, das sich aber auch seiner Herausforderungen bewusst ist. Der Terrorismus durch Boko Haram ist weiterhin eine Gefahr, insbesondere im Norden des Landes, wo die fanatischen Kämpfer junge Mädchen
15 entführen, ihnen Schulbildung verweigern und ganze Landstriche terrorisieren. Es gibt Armut auf dem Land und in der Stadt, und es gibt Hauptstraßen, die sich in der Regenzeit in Flüsse verwandeln und den Verkehr nahezu zum Erliegen bringen. Im Gespräch mit unseren nigerianischen Partnern habe ich dazu ermutigt, bei der Bekämpfung von
20 Menschenhandel und grenzüberschreitender Kriminalität unter Beachtung der Menschenrechte voranzugehen, und ihnen die fortgesetzte Unterstützung Deutschlands und der Europäischen [Union] zugesagt.
From: www.auswaertiges-amt.de, 25 May 2018

Part B
Talking Nigerian

B1 English in Nigeria

About 500 local languages are spoken in Nigeria, but English has the status of an official language. The following statements all deal with the role of English in Nigeria and different attitudes to it.

A

'Oh, yes, you have brought the houseboy. *I kpotago ya.*' Master's Igbo felt feathery in Ugwu's ears. It was Igbo coloured by the sliding sounds of English, the Igbo of one who spoke English often.

From: Chimamanda Adichie: Half of a Yellow Sun, 2007

B

Achebe's decision to write in English has been a source of debate
5 since the beginning of his career, with writers such as the Kenyan author Ngugi wa Thiong'o criticising his use of the colonial language. In 1965 Achebe wrote: 'I feel that the English language will be able to carry the weight of my African experience. But it will have to be a new English, still in full communion with its
10 ancestral home but altered to suit its new African surroundings.' It is a position that he has, broadly, stuck to, although he also points out that some of his best poetry has been first written in Igbo.

From: Nicholas Wroe: 'Chinua Achebe: a life in writing',
The Guardian, 13 December 2010

C

Author and veteran broadcaster, Mrs. Bimbo Oloyede has deplored the poor usage of English Language among Nigerians, particularly
15 journalists, customer service providers, teachers, and even politicians, blaming the development on poor training, illiteracy and influences of dialect. She subsequently tasked experts in the field of English Language to take up the responsibility of guiding the people to speak correctly.
20 [She] noted that as non-native speakers of English Language, Nigerians across major sectors […] require mastery of the language spoken globally to avoid bad influences on their audience, and especially the young ones.

From: Bisi Adewusi: 'Author laments poor use of English language among
Nigerians', The Guardian, 7 June 2018

02 Igbo (also 'Ibo') ['iːbəʊ]: language spoken by the Igbo, an ethnic group living in southern Nigeria (cf. pp. 27–29)
04 Achebe = Chinua Achebe (1930–2013): Nigerian novelist and poet
09 in communion with sth.: connected with sth.
10 ancestral: belonging to people who lived a long time ago
10 alter sth.: change sth.
17 task sb. to do sth. (fml): give sb. the assignment to do sth.

C

I'm not sure my writing in English is a choice. If a Nigerian Igbo like
25 myself is educated exclusively in English, discouraged from
speaking Igbo in a school in which Igbo was just one more subject
of study (and one that was considered 'uncool' by students and did
not receive much support from the administration), then perhaps
writing in English is not a choice, because the idea of choice assumes
30 other equal alternatives. [...]

I write Igbo fairly well, but a lot of my intellectual thinking
cannot be expressed sufficiently in Igbo. Of course, this would be
different if I had been educated in both English and Igbo. [...]

The interesting thing, of course, is that if I did write in Igbo
35 (which I sometimes think of doing, but only for impractical,
emotional reasons), many Igbo people would not be able to read it.
Many educated Igbo people I know can barely read Igbo and they
mostly write it atrociously.

I think that what is more important in this discourse is not
40 whether African writers should or should not write in English but
how African writers, and Africans in general, are educated in
Africa. [...]

I think African writers should write in whatever language they
can. The important thing is to tell African stories. [...] I come from
45 a generation of Nigerians who constantly negotiate two languages
and sometimes three, if you include Pidgin. For the Igbo in
particular, ours is the Engli-Igbo generation and so to somehow
claim that Igbo alone can capture our experience is to limit it.
Globalization has affected us in profound ways.

50 I'd like to say something about English as well, which is simply
that English is mine. Sometimes we talk about English in Africa as
if Africans have no agency, as if there is not a distinct form of English
spoken in Anglophone African countries. I was educated in it; I
spoke it at the same time as I spoke Igbo. My English-speaking is
55 rooted in a Nigerian experience and not in a British or American or
Australian one. I have taken ownership of English.

From: Ada Uzoamaka Azodo: 'Interview with Chimamanda Ngozi Adichie:
Creative writing and literary activism', www.iun.edu, 2008

38 atrocious: very bad
39 discourse: serious
discussion of a topic
46 Pidgin: (here) form of
English used in Nigeria
whose words and grammar
stem from English and
local languages (cf. p. 12)
55 be rooted in sth.: have
its origins in sth.

Comprehension

1 Form groups of 3–4 students, each student dealing with one or two
of the texts above.
  a Make notes on the following aspects:
    – the topic of your text
    – the attitudes to English, to other languages and to the writer's
culture that are expressed in the text (→ Info box, p. 12)

A2 Nigeria's national anthems

1 What is a 'national anthem'? Give a definition.

Info Nigeria's national anthems

Before Nigeria's independence in 1960, the British anthem was sung at important events. The first Nigerian national anthem, 'Nigeria, We Hail Thee' was introduced on Nigerian Independence Day on 1 October, 1960. However, it was met with a number of criticisms, one of them being that it was written by a Briton. Hence, the government launched an open competition for a new anthem. From 1449 suggestions, the lyrics of five different composers were chosen and merged into one final version, 'Arise, O Compatriots', its music being composed by the Nigerian Police Band. It was officially adopted on National Day in 1978. Although it consists of two stanzas, usually only the first one is sung and hence well-known.

Comprehension

Divide the class in two groups. Group A deals with 'Nigeria We Hail Thee', group B with 'Arise, O Compatriots'. Work on tasks **2** and **3**.

2 Read the anthem carefully and mark striking words. Then create a word web to organize your findings and to identify the main topics.

Nigeria We Hail Thee
Lillian Jean Williams
  1. Nigeria we hail thee,
  Our own dear native land,
  Though tribe and tongue may differ,
  In brotherhood we stand,
5 Nigerians all, and proud to serve
  Our sovereign Motherland.

  2. Our flag shall be a symbol
  That truth and justice reign,
  In peace or battle honour'd,
10 And this we count as gain,
  To hand on to our children
  A banner without stain.

  3. O God of all creation,
  Grant this our one request,
15 Help us to build a nation
  Where no man is oppressed,
  And so with peace and plenty
  Nigeria may be blessed.

© 1960 Lillian Jean Williams

Arise, O Compatriots
John A. Ilechukwu et al.
  1. Arise, O compatriots,
  Nigeria's call obey
  To serve our Fatherland
  With love and strength and faith.
5 The labour of our heroes past
  Shall never be in vain,
  To serve with heart and might
  One nation bound in freedom, peace and unity.

10 2. O God of creation,
  Direct our noble cause;
  Guide our Leaders right:
  Help our Youth the truth to know,
  In love and honesty to grow,
15 And living just and true,
  Great lofty heights attain,
  To build a nation where peace
  And justice shall reign.

© 1978 John A. Ilechukwu, Eme Etim Akpan, B. A. Ogunnaike, Sotu Omoigui, P. O. Aderibigbe

Analysis

3 Point out the main message of the anthem and explain how it is underlined by stylistic devices and the choice of words.

> **Language help**
> convey a message · be made up of / consist of … stanzas/verses · use a simple/ colloquial/formal/sophisticated/… register · make use of / employ imagery / personification/alliteration/contrast/repetition/enumeration · illustrate/emphasize/ underline · use similes/metaphors/symbols/specific sentence structures

4 Team up with a partner from the other group.
  a Present your findings to each other, then identify similarities and differences between the anthems. Consider their topics, message and tone.
  b Create a Venn diagram in which you present your findings.

Beyond the text

5 Work on either **a** or **b**.

A Venn diagram

  a Bearing in mind what you have found out about Nigeria's history and the two national anthems, explain what may have made the new anthem more appropriate.
  b Speaking Imagine you're a member of a government committee that has to decide whether to adopt the new anthem. Prepare and give a speech before the committee arguing for or against the anthem.

A3 Post-colonial times

1 You are going to read a short story called 'Civil peace'. Note down your associations with …
  a the title. Consider the individual words and the effect created by combining them.
  b the picture on the right in connection to the title.

The story 'Civil peace' is set right after the end of the Biafran war (→ Info box).

> **Info Biafran War (Nigerian Civil War)**
> The Nigerian Civil War, also called Biafran War, took place from 1967 to 1970 in Biafra, in the south-east of Nigeria, after the dominant Igbo (or Ibo [ˈiːbəʊ]) had declared independence from Nigeria. The war led to fighting and famine in the area, killing about one million people. With British support, Nigeria was victorious over the Igbo in 1970 and reunited the country.

Civil peace *Chinua Achebe*

Jonathan Iwegbu counted himself extra-ordinarily lucky. 'Happy survival!' meant so much more to him than just a current fashion of greeting old friends in the first hazy days of peace. It went deep to his heart. He had come out of the war with five inestimable blessings – his
5   head, his wife Maria's head and the heads of three out of their four children. As a bonus he also had his old bicycle – a miracle too but naturally not to be compared to the safety of five human heads.

The bicycle had a little history of its own. One day at the height of the war it was commandeered 'for urgent military action'. Hard as its
10   loss would have been to him he would still have let it go without a thought had he not had some doubts about the genuineness of the officer. It wasn't his disreputable rags, nor the toes peeping out of one blue and one brown canvas shoes, nor yet the two stars of his rank done obviously in a hurry in biro, that troubled Jonathan; many good and
15   heroic soldiers looked the same or worse. It was rather a certain lack of grip and firmness in his manner. So Jonathan, suspecting he might be amenable to influence, rummaged in his raffia bag and produced the two pounds with which he had been going to buy firewood which his wife, Maria, retailed to camp officials for extra stock-fish and corn meal,
20   and got his bicycle back. That night he buried it in the little clearing in the bush where the dead of the camp, including his own youngest son, were buried. When he dug it up again a year later after the surrender all it needed was a little palm-oil greasing. 'Nothing puzzles God,' he said in wonder.
25   He put it to immediate use as a taxi and accumulated a small pile of Biafran money ferrying camp officials and their families across the four-mile stretch to the nearest tarred road. His standard charge per trip was six pounds and those who had the money were only glad to be rid of some of it in this way. At the end of a fortnight he had made a
30   small fortune of one hundred and fifteen pounds.

Then he made the journey to Enugu and found another miracle waiting for him. It was unbelievable. He rubbed his eyes and looked again and it was still standing there before him. But, needless to say, even that monumental blessing must be accounted also totally inferior
35   to the five heads in the family. This newest miracle was his little house in Ogui Overside. Indeed nothing puzzles God! Only two houses away a huge concrete edifice some wealthy contractor had put up just before the war was a mountain of rubble. And here was Jonathan's little zinc house of no regrets built with mud blocks quite intact! Of course the
40   doors and windows were missing and five sheets off the roof.

But what was that? And anyhow he had returned to Enugu early enough to pick up bits of old zinc and wood and soggy sheets of cardboard lying around the neighbourhood before thousands more came out of their forest holes looking for the same things. He got a destitute

3 hazy: foggy
4 inestimable: valuable
9 commandeer sth.: take control of sth. for military purposes during war
11 genuineness: trustworthiness
12 disreputable: (here) untidy
12 rags: old, torn clothes
13 canvas: rough material used by painters for painting on
14 biro (BE): plastic pen
16 grip: power
17 amenable to sth.: (here) open to sth.
19 retail sth. to sb.: sell sth. to sb.
23 greasing: act of rubbing fat on sth. in order to make it run smoothly
29 fortnight: two weeks
34 account sth. as sth. else (fml): consider sth. as sth. else
37 edifice: large impressive building
37 contractor: company that carries out work for others
38 rubble: broken stones or bricks
38 zinc: *Wellblech*
42 soggy: wet
44 destitute: poor

45 carpenter with one old hammer, a blunt plane and a few bent and rusty nails in his tool bag to turn this assortment of wood, paper and metal into door and window shutters for five Nigerian shillings or fifty Biafran pounds. He paid the pounds, and moved in with his overjoyed family carrying five heads on their shoulders.

50   His children picked mangoes near the military cemetery and sold them to soldiers' wives for a few pennies – real pennies this time – and his wife started making breakfast akara balls for neighbours in a hurry to start life again. With his family earnings he took his bicycle to the villages around and bought fresh palm-wine which he mixed generously 55 in his rooms with the water which had recently started running again in the public tap down the road, and opened up a bar for soldiers and other lucky people with good money.

    At first he went daily, then every other day and finally once a week, to the offices of the Coal Corporation where he used to be a miner, to 60 find out what was what. The only thing he did find out in the end was that that little house of his was even a greater blessing than he had thought. Some of his fellow ex-miners who had nowhere to return at the end of the day's waiting just slept outside the doors of the offices and cooked what meal they could scrounge together in Bournvita tins. 65 As the weeks lengthened and still nobody could say what was what Jonathan discontinued his weekly visits altogether and faced his palm-wine bar.

    But nothing puzzles God. Came the day of the windfall when after five days of endless scuffles in queues and counter-queues in the sun 70 outside the Treasury he had twenty pounds counted into his palms as exgratia award for the rebel money he had turned in. It was like Christmas for him and for many others like him when the payments began. They called it (since few could manage its proper official name) egg-rasher.

    As soon as the pound notes were placed in his palm Jonathan simply 75 closed it tight over them and buried fist and money inside his trouser pocket. He had to be extra careful because he had seen a man a couple of days earlier collapse into near-madness in an instant before that oceanic crowd because no sooner had he got his twenty pounds than some heartless ruffian picked it off him. Though it was not right that a 80 man in such an extremity of agony should be blamed yet many in the queues that day were able to remark quietly on the victim's carelessness, especially after he pulled out the innards of his pocket and revealed a hole in it big enough to pass a thief's head. But of course he had insisted that the money had been in the other pocket, pulling it out too to show 85 its comparative wholeness. So one had to be careful.

    Jonathan soon transferred the money to his left hand and pocket so as to leave his right free for shaking hands should the need arise, though by fixing his gaze at such an elevation as to miss all approaching human faces he made sure that the need did not arise, until he got home.

45 blunt: unsharpened
45 plane: *Hobel*
52 akara: fried cake made of mashed black-eyed peas
64 scrounge sth.: get sth. for free by asking sb. for it
68 windfall: sum of money you receive unexpectedly
69 scuffle (n): struggle
71 exgratia (= ex gratia) award: prize given as a favour not because you are obliged to do it
78 no sooner ... than ...: *kaum, dass ...*
79 ruffian: violent man
80 agony: suffering
88 fix your gaze at such an elevation as to ...: fix your eyes at such a height that ...

90　He was normally a heavy sleeper but that night he heard all the neighbourhood noises die down one after another. Even the night watchman who knocked the hour on some metal somewhere in the distance had fallen silent after knocking one o'clock. That must have been the last thought in Jonathan's mind before he was finally carried

95　away himself. He couldn't have been gone for long, though, when he was violently awakened again.

'Who is knocking?' whispered his wife lying beside him on the floor.

'I don't know,' he whispered back breathlessly.

The second time the knocking came it was so loud and imperious

100　that the rickety old door could have fallen down.

'Who is knocking?' he asked then, his voice parched and trembling.

'Na tief-man and him people,' came the cool reply. 'Make you hopen de door.' This was followed by the heaviest knocking of all.

105　Maria was the first to raise the alarm, then he followed and all their children.

'Police-o! Thieves-o! Neighbours-o! Police-o! We are lost! We are dead! Neighbours, are you asleep? Wake up! Police-o!'

This went on for a long time and then stopped suddenly. Perhaps

110　they had scared the thief away. There was total silence. But only for a short while.

'You done finish?' asked the voice outside. 'Make we help you small. Oya, everybody!'

'Police-o! Tief-man-o! Neighbours-o! we done loss-o! Police-o! ...'

115　There were at least five other voices besides the leader's.

Jonathan and his family were now completely paralysed by terror. Maria and the children sobbed inaudibly like lost souls. Jonathan groaned continuously.

The silence that followed the thieves' alarm vibrated horribly. Jonathan

120　all but begged their leader to speak again and be done with it.

'My frien,' said he at long last, 'we don try our best for call dem but I tink say dem all done sleep-o ... So wetin we go do now? Sometaim you wan call soja? Or you wan make we call dem for you? Soja better pass police. No be so?'

125　'Na so!' replied his men. Jonathan thought he heard even more voices now than before and groaned heavily. His legs were sagging under him and his throat felt like sandpaper.

'My frien, why you no de talk again. I de ask you say you wan make we call soja?'

130　'No'.

'Awrighto. Now make we talk business. We no be bad tief. We no like for make trouble. Trouble done finish. War done finish and all the katakata wey de for inside. No Civil War again. This time na Civil Peace. No be so?'

99 imperious [ɪmˈpɪərɪəs]: (here) aggressive
101 parched: dry
103 tief-man (Nigerian Pidgin): thief
107 -o (Nigerian Pidgin): suffix added put emphasis on a word
113 oya (Nigerian Pidgin): hurry up
117 inaudible: impossible to hear
118 groan: make a long deep sound from pain or discomfort
123 soja (Nigerian Pidgin): soldier
126 sag (v): become weaker
133 katakata (Nigerian Pidgin): problem, trouble

135 'Na so!' answered the horrible chorus.

'What do you want from me? I am a poor man. Everything I had went with this war. Why do you come to me? You know people who have money. We ...'

'Awright! We know say you no get plenty money. But we sef no get
140 even anini. So derefore make you open dis window and give us one hundred pound and we go commot. Orderwise we de come for inside now to show you guitar-boy like dis ...'

A volley of automatic fire rang through the sky. Maria and the children began to weep aloud again.

145 'Ah, missisi de cry again. No need for dat. We done talk say we na good tief. We just take our small money and go nwayorly. No molest. Abi we de molest?'

'At all!' sang the chorus.

'My friends,' began Jonathan hoarsely. 'I hear what you say and I
150 thank you. If I had one hundred pounds ...'

'Lookia my frien, no be play we come play for your house. If we make mistake and step for inside you no go like am-o. So derefore ...'

'To God who made me; if you come inside and find one hundred pounds, take it and shoot me and shoot my wife and children. I swear
155 to God. The only money I have in this life is this twenty-pounds egg-rasher they gave me today ...'

'OK. Time de go. Make you open dis window and bring the twenty pound. We go manage am like dat.'

There were now loud murmurs of dissent among the chorus: 'Na lie
160 de man de lie; e get plenty money ... Make we go inside and search properly well ... Wetin be twenty pound? ...'

'Shurrup!' rang the leader's voice like a lone shot in the sky and silenced the murmuring at once. 'Are you dere? Bring the money quick!'

'I am coming,' said Jonathan fumbling in the darkness with the key
165 of the small wooden box he kept by his side on the mat.

At the first sign of light as neighbours and others assembled to commiserate with him he was already strapping his five-gallon demijohn to his bicycle carrier and his wife, sweating in the open fire, was turning over akara balls in a wide clay bowl of boiling oil. In the corner his eldest
170 son was rinsing out dregs of yesterday's palm wine from old beer bottles.

'I count it as nothing,' he told his sympathizers, his eyes on the rope he was tying. 'What is egg-rasher? Did I depend on it last week? Or is it greater than other things that went with the war? I say, let egg-rasher
175 perish in the flames! Let it go where everything else has gone. Nothing puzzles God.'

From: Chinua Achebe, Girls at War and Other Stories, *1972*

139 sef (Nigerian Pidgin): safe
140 anini (Nigerian Pidgin): any
147 molest sb.: abuse sb.
147 abi (Nigerian Pidgin): Is it true?
149 hoarse (adj): sounding rough
159 dissent (n): disagreement
167 commiserate with sb.: show sb. sympathy
167 demijohn: bottle
170 dregs: the last drops of a liquid
175 perish: die

Akara balls

Comprehension

2 a Answer the *w*-questions in the diagram.

why _____

how _____   who _____

_____   ↻

_____ what   when _____

where _____

b Describe the atmosphere in Jonathan's hometown.

c Language plays an essential role in 'Civil peace'. Although you have probably never heard the words from Nigerian Pidgin (cf. p. 12) or Igbo used in the text, you will easily understand them. Choose three examples and translate them into British English.

Analysis

3 a Analyse the structure of the short story. Identify the typical elements of exposition, rising action, climax, falling action, resolution. Draw a graph containing these elements and key events from the story.

b Describe Jonathan's character.

Language help

… is presented/portrayed as … · the writer characterizes … as … · … appears to be … · His behaviour shows/indicates … · The way he talks implies that … · This proves that … is a person who can be considered as optimistic/pessimistic/trustworthy/strong/ humble/outgoing/shy/ambitious

c Analyse whether Achebe uses direct or indirect means to characterize Jonathan (→ Info box). Give examples.

Info Characterization

Direct/explicit characterization: The reader is told about a character's personality directly by the narrator, another character or the character him- or herself.
Indirect/implicit characterization: The reader is expected to draw conclusions about a character by studying his or her behaviour, opinions, choice of words and/or way of talking.

d Achebe also makes use of language to characterize Jonathan and the thieves. Explain who uses Nigerian Pidgin / Igbo, British English and religious expressions and why.

4 Go back to your results from task **1**.

   a Assess to what extent your associations with the bike fit the story.

   b Assess to what extent your associations with the title 'Civil peace' fit the story. Explain the title.

Beyond the text

5 In a magazine article Lagosians are described as especially optimistic and courageous (cf. p. 37 f.). Is this also true of Jonathan? Work on either task **a** or **b**.

   a `Writing` Write one or two paragraphs of an article discussing the question.

   b `Speaking` Discuss the question with a partner: Partner A argues in favour of, partner B against the idea. Collect arguments for your position and think of ways to refute your partner's arguments, then hold the discussion.

6 `Writing` Five years later, Jonathan sends a letter to a friend in Lagos. He tells him about the current situation in his hometown, his family and life. Write Jonathan's letter.

A4 Muhammadu Buhari's inauguration

In 2015, Muhammadu Buhari from the All Progress Congress Party won the presidential elections against Goodluck Jonathan, former president in office and member of the People's Democratic Party. Buhari was sworn in on 29 May 2015.

Muhammadu Buhari at his second inauguration ceremony in 2019

1 `Viewing` Watch the video without sound.

   a For each scene of the video, make notes on its setting, as well as the people and the actions shown.

   b Describe the atmosphere at the ceremony. Choose two of the following adjectives and explain your choice. Which other adjectives can you think of?

Video online:
cornelsen.de
Code: wuceje

cheerful · cold · hopeless · depressing · gloomy · formal · friendly · hopeful · informative · liberating · optimistic · overwhelming · pessimistic · relaxed · tense · violent

2 `Viewing` Watch the video with sound (→ Annotations).

Video online:
cornelsen.de
Code: wuceje

Annotations
- swear sb. in: admit sb. to an important office
- incumbent: person who currently holds an official position

a Finish the following sentence beginnings.

A The inauguration ceremony is …

_____

B When Buhari moves around the square …

_____

C It is a historic time for Nigeria because …

_____

D International leaders are hoping that despite a fiercely fought election there can be …

_____

E The people's message for President Buhari is that they are …

_____

F On Buhari's to-do list as president is …

_____

b Reconsider your results from task **1b**: would you change your mind after listening to the video with sound? Why (not)?

Beyond the text

3 Do some research on Muhammadu Buhari. Collect information on him as a person as well as on his political policy, then work on task **a**, **b** or **c**.

a `Writing` Imagine how Buhari would present himself. Create a social media site for Buhari.

b `Speaking` Work with a partner. Write a TV interview with suitable questions and answers given by Buhari. Film your interview to create a 90-second video.

c `Writing` Imagine you are a young Nigerian and see the video from task **2**. Leave a short message on the website in which you either …
- comment on Buhari's plans for Nigeria's future or
- present your Nigerian dream (e. g. What does your country stand for? What do you want to be proud of?) and describe how Buhari has contributed to it.

Part B
Nigeria and Nigerians

B1 Nigerian people

Nigeria has always been populated by many different ethnic groups.
You are going to learn about three of them.

Info Ethnic diversity in Nigeria
Being a multi-ethnic nation, Nigeria is
home to more than 250 ethnic groups.
The three largest are the Hausa-Fulani,
who live mostly in the north, the Igbo
(or Ibo ['iːbəʊ]), who are predominant in
the south-east, and the Yoruba ['_ _ _]
in the south-west. Together, they account
for roughly 68 per cent of the population.
The rest of Nigeria's ethnic groups live
all over the country. The ethnic identity
of each individual group usually centres
around a common language, around
shared religion, values, traditions and
customs (e. g. in terms of food,
traditional clothing, forms of address).

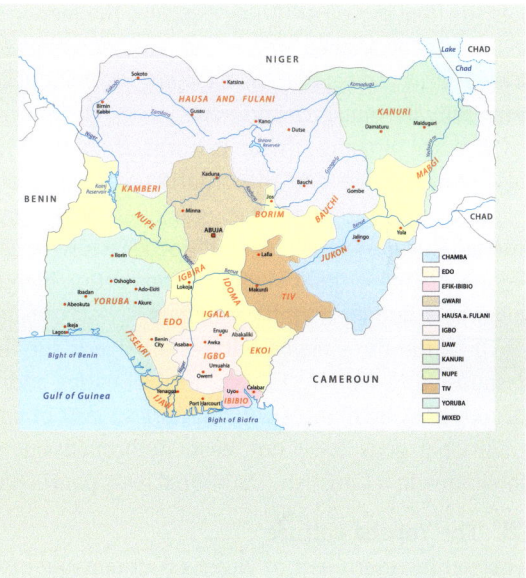

Comprehension

Divide the class into three groups, each of them reading one of the
book excerpts below and working on task **1**.
1 In your expert group, collect information about …
  – your ethnic group's situation today and
  – the factors contributing to this situation.
  Discuss your findings, focusing on what it means to be an I(g)bo,
  Yoruba or Hausa today. Make sure you are able to present your
  results to other students.

A **The Ibo culture** *William Drake*

The Ibos dominate in five states in southeastern Nigeria – Abia, Enugu,
Imo, Anambra and Ebonyi. They have a long tradition of both agriculture
and business, and have a reputation as very capable traders. There are
strong cultural values of fairness and honesty among themselves,
whether in the marketplace or in politics – in both of these arenas a
clever strategy for success in business or politics is universally admired
while the corrupt exercise of power is not.

The Ibos are known as independent free-thinkers, which may have something to do with the fact that their supreme rulers, the 'Eze' or
10 kings, have never been as all-powerful as the rulers of the other two major cultures, the Yoruba and the Hausa. Whereas in Yorubaland and Hausaland one-man rule is the norm, in Iboland there is a long history of indigenous democratic processes.

The British colonials, whose strategy was always to co-opt the top
15 leadership and to control the people through those leaders, found their strategy didn't work that well in Iboland, where no single person ever has the final say on anything – except the man in his own house, and even then Ibo women are not that easily dominated at home and have a well-deserved reputation for being strong and independent people
20 especially in commerce and trade.

Atypical of many African cultures, even in his home the Ibo man is more consultative than authoritarian – although of course personality plays a role in this on the individual level. However, in most Ibo communities no man is allowed to go too far toward being an authoritarian
25 figure at home without vigorous intervention by both extended family, neighbors, and community members.

Of all the three major cultures of Nigeria the Ibos have been most responsive to western Christian missionaries and today the majority of Ibos are Christians – with an African flair of course, because their
30 traditional gods have not been dethroned but instead have been integrated in a Christian/traditional gods pantheon. […]

B The Yoruba culture

The southwestern part of Nigeria is dominated by the Yoruba people, and includes the great city of Lagos and the states of Lagos, Ondo, Ogun,
35 Osun, Ekiti and Oyo. However since Lagos is the commercial capital of Nigeria, and is arguably the greatest commercial center in Africa, every culture is represented in the city and to a large extent it is actually dominated by Ibo people. The Yoruba people have a vast and complex pantheon of traditional gods and deities and have also accepted both
40 Christianity and Islam alongside their traditional religious concepts.

Christian missionaries had strong early success among the Yoruba, as did the messengers of Islam, and many observers have noted that the Yoruba seem to be fascinated with anything new in the spiritual realm and are almost always early-adopters in this area. The Yoruba are
45 very much controlled by their hierarchical rulers, the 'Oba', who in many cases exercise absolute authority, a factor that allowed the British colonials to successfully co-opt the traditional rulers and govern through them.

This centralized authority also made the Yoruba vulnerable to
50 enslavement and sale by their own rulers, and today the descendants

14 co-opt sb.: bring sb. over to your side, gaining their help
22 consultative: giving advice
22 authoritarian [ɔːˌθɒrɪ'teəriən]: strict
25 vigorous: energetic
30 dethrone sb.: remove sb. from power
31 pantheon: assembly of the gods
39 deity ['deɪəti]: god/goddess
43 realm [relm]: (here) sphere
49 vulnerable to sth.: likely to be influenced by sth.
50 enslavement: act of making sb. a slave
50 descendant [dɪ'sendənt]: sb.'s children and all the following generations

of Yoruba slaves dominate the African-American populations of all Western countries where slavery was an historical abomination.

Yoruba men tend to rule their households in an authoritarian manner the same way that Yoruba society itself is governed. There is also
55 a strong polygamous family model in Yoruba society that can be at least partly understood as a man's need to demonstrate strength and authority by having several wives and numerous children – his own little kingdom, so to speak. The polygamous model is still quite strong in rural areas, but is breaking down to some extent in the cities largely
60 because of the economic limitations of having multiple spouses and many children to support, as well as the rapid emergence of social consciousness and personal confidence among Yoruba women. […]

C The Hausa culture

The Hausa dominate the entire Northern part of Nigeria and Hausaland
65 is by far the greatest in territory and population of the three dominant cultures. […]

There are very few large cities in Hausaland, but the two principal cities Kano and Kaduna are thriving commercial centers. However, most of the Hausa live in small agricultural villages surrounded by farms and
70 grazing lands. The Hausa are Islamic and are dominated politically and religiously by powerful absolute rulers called Emirs whose word is basically the law and who are supported by an almost equally powerful council of clergy called the 'Mallamai', whose job is to strictly enforce the will of the Emir and Sharia Law, the strict and some would say
75 fundamentalist legal structure imposed by conservative Islam.

Keeping in line with the fundamental teachings of conservative Islam, Muslim leaders have historically resisted (to put it mildly) Christian attempts to penetrate the North. There are numerous branches of Nigerian Islam, including Sunnis, Ahmadiyuo, Bori, Quadiriya,
80 and Tijaniya.

Because of the strict hierarchical nature of the Hausa they were easily dominated by the British colonials, who simply co-opted the few at the top and thereby ruled from behind the scenes with absolute authority. Women have always been very much second-class citizens among the
85 Hausa, rarely allowed to work or obtain an education, and basically serve as house slaves for their husbands, who by tradition have more than one wife and, if they can afford it, one or more mistresses as well.

From: William Drake, Understanding Nigerian Culture through American Eyes, *2018*

2 Get together in groups of three, with each member having worked on a different excerpt.

  a Speaking Present your findings to each other.

  b Make a graphic organizer (e. g. word web, concept map) visualizing ethnic diversity in Nigeria.

52 abomination: scandal
55 polygamous [ˈ _ _ _] having more than one wife at the same time
60 spouse: partner in marriage
61 emergence: appearance
68 thrive: be successful
73 clergy ['klɜːdʒi]: priests

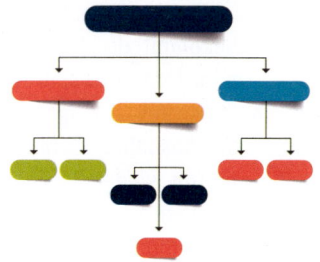

Analysis

3 Examine the article's tone. (→ Info box)

> **Info Tone**
>
> The tone of a text is the way that a writer treats his or her topic and it reveals his or her attitude towards it and also towards the reader. Elements such as diction (i. e. choice of words), syntax, speaker and imagery can influence the tone of a text. The tone can be e. g. intimate, detached, distanced, angry, solemn, informal, jocular, serious, ironic, humorous, neutral.

Beyond the text

4 `Speaking` In your groups, discuss what your findings from task **1** could mean for a Nigerian's identity today.

5 `Writing` Comment on the way the three ethnicities are presented in the text. Refer to your results from task **3** and consider the writer's origin.

B2 Nigerian-German relations

In October 2016 then German Foreign Minister Frank-Walter Steinmeier paid a state visit to Nigeria.

1 `Mediating` Imagine you are former Nigerian ambassador Rimdap (cf. l. 47) and give a speech in parliament on the relationship between Nigeria and Germany. On the basis of the article, illustrate their current relationship and point out why their future cooperation will be of great importance for both countries.

Das „Powerhouse" Afrikas *Adrian Kriesch*

Das „Powerhouse" Afrikas – so nennt der deutsche Außenminister zum Auftakt sein Reiseziel Nigeria. Frank-Walter Steinmeier verweist auf den Ressourcenreichtum und die Bevölkerungszahl, mit rund 180 Millionen Einwohnern ist Nigeria das bevölkerungsreichste Land
5 des Kontinents. Das Wort „Powerhouse" scheint dem Außenminister zu gefallen, auf seiner Facebook-Seite wirft er regelrecht damit um sich.

Doch Afrikas „Powerhouse" hat gewaltige Probleme. Steinmeier bekommt das gleich selbst beim Besuch im nigerianischen Außenministerium zu spüren. Kurz bevor er in den Fahrstuhl steigt, fällt der
10 Strom aus. „No light", sagen ihm die Nigerianer – das ist hier eher Regel aus Ausnahme. Schließlich sind die Generatoren eingeschaltet, das Licht brennt wieder. Als Steinmeier im achten Stockwerk auf seinen nigerianischen Amtskollegen Geoffrey Onyeama trifft, geht im Gespräch die Aufreihung der Probleme weiter: Wirtschaftskrise, Terrorismus,
15 Korruption, Flüchtlingskrise. [...]

Zwei Millionen Euro für Nothilfe im Nordosten

49 DW: Deutsche Welle

Mit Blick auf die Sicherheitslage und den Kampf gegen Boko Haram im Nordosten des Landes sagt Steinmeier weitere Unterstützung zu. Zwar geht das nigerianische Militär in den letzten Monaten relativ erfolgreich
20 gegen die Terroristen vor, doch die humanitäre Krise spitzt sich zu. Mehr als zwei Millionen Menschen wurden durch den Terror vertrieben. Das Kinderhilfswerk UNICEF warnt, dass 400 000 Kinder unter fünf Jahren unter lebensbedrohlicher Mangelernährung leiden und fordert dringend mehr Geld. Auch die Kanzlerin hat vor ihrer Afrika-Reise unter-
25 finanzierte UN-Projekte in der Region um den Tschadsee angesprochen, Steinmeier hat in Abuja nun zusätzlich zwei Millionen Euro dafür zugesagt. Insgesamt finanziert das Auswärtige Amt dieses Jahr in der Region humanitäre Projekte mit 18,7 Millionen Euro. Ab nächstem Jahr soll außerdem ein Ausbildungsprogramm für die Polizei finanziert wer-
30 den. Beobachter in Nigeria kritisieren immer wieder, dass das Militär überlastet sei, da die Polizei im Nordosten kaum noch ihren Aufgaben nachkommt – selbst in den zurückeroberten Gebieten.

Neue Freunde in Afrika

Ist das „Powerhouse" Nigeria also nur noch ein einziger Flächenbrand?
35 Nein, Steinmeier sieht Lichtblicke: der demokratische Machtwechsel im Land, der entschlossene Kampf gegen Korruption und gegen Boko Haram. Auch die Beziehungen zwischen Nigeria und Deutschland seien hervorragend. Das zeigen die vielen gegenseitigen Besuche – Ende der Woche wird der nigerianische Präsident Buhari in Berlin Kanzlerin
40 Merkel treffen – und auch die dritte Tagung einer binationalen Kommission, die anlässlich der Steinmeier-Reise stattfand. Seit 2011 diskutieren dabei Expertengruppen beider Länder. „Unzählige Projekte" seien dabei angestoßen worden, so Steinmeier. Viel Konkretes ist jedoch nicht an die Öffentlichkeit gedrungen.
45 „Wir merken, dass Deutschland Afrika gerade stark auf dem Radar hat", sagt Nigerias Außenminister und lobt die Zusammenarbeit. Das sei auch höchste Zeit, meint Abdulkadir Bin Rimdap, ehemaliger Botschafter Nigerias in Deutschland, am Rande des Steinmeier-Besuches gegenüber der DW. „Deutschland war mal auf Platz drei der füh-
50 renden Wirtschaftsnationen auf der Welt, jetzt ist es auf Platz fünf. Ihr solltet also besser schnell neue Freunde in Afrika suchen", so Rimdap. Weniger als 90 deutsche Firmen sind bisher im bevölkerungsreichsten Land Afrikas aktiv. Das spricht weder für den Wirtschaftsmotor Deutschland, noch für das „Powerhouse" Nigeria.

From: the website of Deutsche Welle, *11 October 2016*

Chapter III

Voices from Nigeria

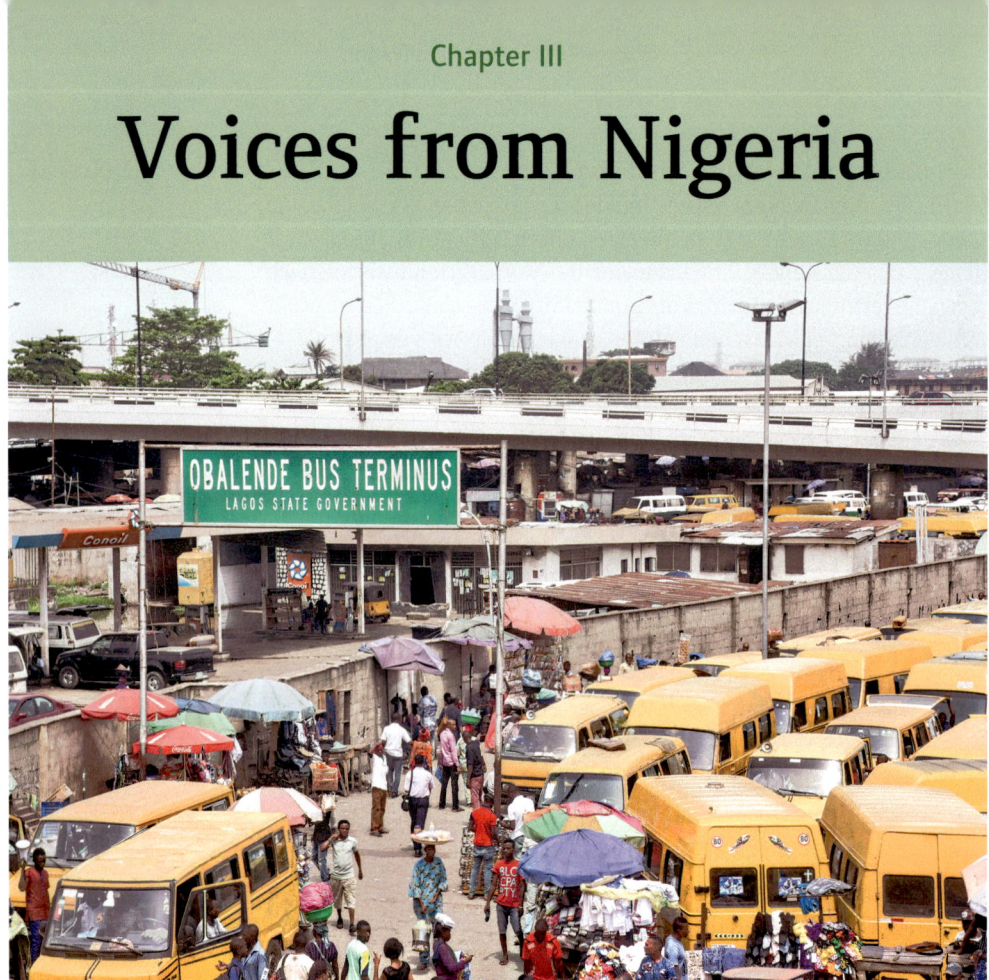

Part A
Lagos – city of optimists?

A1 Impressions of Lagos

With its 22 million inhabitants, Nigeria's 'secret capital' Lagos is its most populous city and one of the fastest growing cities worldwide.

1 The photo above shows Obalende bus stop in Lagos (→ Info box Obalende, p. 33). Choose a particular spot in the photo that you find interesting. Imagine standing at that spot and describe …
  – what you can see, hear and smell
  – what the people around you are doing
  – what you know about those people
  – what might have brought you and/or the other people to Lagos
  – how you feel.
Make notes. Don't think too much; decide and write on impulse.

> **Info Obalende**
>
> The photo on p. 32 shows Obalende bus stop and market area in Lagos. Strategically placed close to influential and wealthy Lagos Island (or simply 'The island', as the local government area is called), it is one of the city's major transportation hubs. Many interstate buses from around the country arrive and you can hop on buses taking you to virtually every part of the city. Obalende is also famous for its vibrant activity taking place 24/7.

2 Share ideas with a partner. Ask questions about their experiences and be ready to answer theirs. Collect as many ideas as possible.

A2 Destination: Lagos (1)

The two following fictional texts in **A2** and **A3** deal with people either on their way to Lagos or about to leave for Lagos.

Chike is on the run. He was a soldier in the Nigerian army fighting against the militants in the Niger Delta, and he deserted because he could no longer stand the atrocities ordered by his superiors. On a bus to Lagos he sits next to a woman called Ifeoma.

Lagos

Hope *Chibundu Onuzo*

He turned off his torch and put the Bible away. How long till Lagos? It was like London, they said, everything was new and expensive. Big cars, models you would never see anywhere else in Nigeria. Large houses. Money everywhere. And under these fantastic stories of riches, always
5 a layer of unease: of daylight robberies and mysterious disappearances.

The woman beside him no longer breathed evenly. She gave no other sign she was awake. Her arm remained resting on his, where it had fallen in her sleep. She was crying, he realized.

'Excuse me, is everything alright?' Chike asked.
10 'I thought everyone was asleep.'

'Do you need a light?'

'I've found what I'm looking for.'

She blew her nose softly, the mucus sliding out in a rasp. He laid his head on the window again and watched the road. A few moments later,
15 she began to cry again.

'Are you sure there's nothing I can do for you?'

'I'm tired, but this man's driving won't let me sleep. And I checked before getting on the bus. He looked responsible. How am I going to manage till Lagos?'
20 'Will it be your first time in the city?' he asked?

'No, but I can't wait to arrive. I tire for this Niger Delta. It's so dangerous these days. Once you step out of your house, you're afraid. If it's not kidnapping, it's armed robbery or assassination.'

5 unease: feeling of being worried about sth.
13 mucus ['mjuːkəs]: thick slime coming out your nose when you have a cold
21 tire for sth.: (here) get tired of sth.
23 assassination: planned murder of a person, especially an important person

'Yes,' Chike said. 'It's becoming something else. I hope you don't mind
25 my asking but if I was trying to find somewhere reasonable to stay in
Lagos, where would you advise?'

'You can try Ojota or Ketu. That's around where I'll be staying.
I haven't even told my cousin I'm arriving tomorrow. I called her number
but it's not going through.

30 'Do you have an address?' Chike asked?

'Yes of course. I just hope she won't turn me away.'

'I'm sure she won't.'

'Why are you so sure? Nobody knows I'm going to Lagos,' she said,
her voice suddenly cracking in a sob. 'I'm running away.'

35 Chike was the one who had drawn her out in conversation and now
he wished he had left her to her tears. 'My husband beats me. Often.
My mother said I should prepare his favourite soup for him, ofe nsala
with plenty stockfish. My brother says I should beg him. They've all
told me to stay. Stay so the police can discover my dead body.' […]

40 'I can tell you my own secret,' Chike said. 'Grown man like me, I'm
scared of Lagos.'

'Why? Because there are so many Yorubas?'

'And how do you know I'm not Yoruba?'

'You just have this Igbo look about you.' […] 'As for me', she
45 continued, 'the first time I arrived in Lagos, stepping down at the
motor park was a shock. I grew up in the East so to have everybody
crowding around you, speaking this language you don't understand,
I fear o. Somebody can sell you in the market, you won't know.'

'I speak enough Yoruba but Lagos just has this reputation.'

50 'Armed robbers. Ritual killers. Drug dealers. It's like that and it's not
like that. I always enjoy my visits. There's something always happening
there. Ngwanu, let us sleep. You don't want to be tired when you get
to Lagos. Good night.'

'Thanks. Good night.'

55 Chike put his temple on the window and continued to watch the road.
A year ago, he would never have believed he could leave the army, so
set was he in the routine of military life. Yet here he was on his way to
Lagos. He was not too old adopt and adapt new methods. There was a
new life waiting for him in Lagos. He would make his way.

From: Welcome to Lagos, *2017*

43 Yoruba ['_ _ _]: person
from an ethnic group
living in the Nigerian
southwest (cf. pp. 27–29)
44 Igbo (also 'Ibo')
['iːbəʊ]: belonging to the
Igbo people, an ethnic
group living predomin-
antly in the southeast of
Nigeria (cf. pp. 27–29)
48 I fear o: In Nigerian
Pidgin English, the sound
'o' is often placed at
the end of sentences
for emphasis.
52 Ngwanu (Igbo):
Oh well!

Comprehension

1 **Speaking** Imagine you had sat on the bus behind Chike and Ifeoma.
Summarize their conversation by telling somebody else what they
talked about.

2 Point out what is driving Ifeoma away from home. Differentiate
between general aspects regarding her hometown or region and her
domestic situation.

Analysis

3 Identify the different facets of Lagos presented in the text by copying and completing the table below. Also include aspects only hinted at. Don't forget to give line numbers.

Hopes	Fears and dangers
maybe like London (cf. l. 6)	feeling of unease (cf. l. 9)
new, expensive (cf. l. 6)	daylight robberies (cf. l. 9)
…	…

Beyond the text

4 Comment on Ifeoma's enigmatic statement in l. 51f. ('It's … that').

5 Writing On the basis of your findings, write a characterization of Lagos for a travel guide. Use a dictionary to find suitable adjectives in order to create a vivid image of the city.

A3 Destination: Lagos (2)

Chief Sandayo, Nigeria's Minister of Education, is presently living in Nigeria's capital Abuja. He has just found out that he is about to be dismissed from office.

Home *Chibundu Onuzo*

He cancelled all his meetings that day and returned to his mansion, large with small block windows that gave the building a squint. It was an ugly house built on land worth its weight in government contracts. He had little there: a few suitcases, some paintings from his Lagos home,
5 his favourite armchair. It was not his house, only a loan from the government until his ministerial term was up. And yet, it could so easily have belonged to him. These things could all be arranged, as could all the other suspect perks of being a minister in Abuja.

He climbed upstairs to his room. The house was empty, his maid and
10 cook gone God knows where. He did not often return this early. He lay flat on the four-poster bed staring at the brocade canopy embroidered with birds in flight. His wife would have hated this master bedroom. It was lit by yellow bulbs that glowed garish from the chandelier. Funkẹ had loved natural light so much, she had designed large glass windows
15 for every room of their house in Lagos, glass windows that had to be covered with metal sheets at night, except for the window of their bedroom, a single bulletproof pane that let her watch the sun rise.

1 mansion: very large, expensive house
2 give sth. a squint: make sth. look malformed
6 term: period of time during which someone is in a position
6 be up: be over
8 suspect [ˈ_ _]: dubious, possibly illegal
8 perks (pl): sth. you are given for a job in addition to your salary
11 four-poster bed: large bed with four solid posts in each corner
11 canopy: (here) large piece of cloth spread over the bed like a roof
11 embroider sth.: *etwas besticken*
13 garish: too bright
17 bulletproof pane: piece of glass in a window that is strong enough to withstand gunfire

He certainly would not wait to be fired. He would return to his well-lit Lagos home with his suitcases and his
20 armchair and his paintings especially. On the wall hung his favourite Grillo, an indigo long-necked woman, her gele opening like petals around her inscrutable face. It reminded him of Funkẹ when they first met: the elegant, almost scrawny neck, the flamboyant clothes, the pervading
25 mystery in everything she said and did.

Abuja

If his wife were alive, he would never have taken this job. She hated Abuja with its sterile parks and lit-up avenues, wide freeways that led nowhere. And behind this ordered, meticulous cleanliness, the most unjust, most grotesque, most perverse of transactions. No, Funkẹ's puritan
30 sensibilities would not have withstood the capital and he would not have come without her.

Theirs, in the beginning, had been a fairy tale. The village boy from Ikire; the Lagos girl with no concept of lack. She had not been the most beautiful but she had embodied his aspirations with her foreign
35 education and the English surname he almost regretted her exchanging for his own. And then she had some sort of experience in a church, a vision, a blinding light, an angelic visitation that had changed her. Stopped drinking. Stopped swearing. Begun building celestial houses, four-storey mansions in the sky. It was partly why he had been driven
40 to the YPC where the goals where more solid

Their marriage had broken down long before he buried her but they had never lived apart. No matter how far he strayed, Funkẹ remained under his roof, a pious, holy, chanting talisman. He would return to the house she had designed at the height of their love for each other, a
45 mansion charming in its unevenness. Let them keep their Abuja. He was going home to Lagos.

From: Welcome to Lagos*, 2017*

21 Grillo = John Grillo (1917–2014): US-American painter
21 gele: African head-wrap typically covering a woman's entire hair
22 petal ['petl]: *Blütenblatt*
22 inscrutable: mysterious
24 scrawny: very thin
24 flamboyant: brightly coloured and easily noticed
28 meticulous: very careful and thorough
33 lack (n): state of not having sth.
34 aspiration: hope to have or achieve sth.
37 angelic [æn'dʒelɪk]: like an angel
38 celestial: heavenly
40 YPC = Yoruba Peoples Congress, political institution of the Yoruba people of southwestern Nigeria
43 pious ['paɪəs]: very religious

Comprehension
1 Summarize the text in no more than 150 words.

Analysis
2 Point out Chief Sandayo's attitude toward Abuja and his home there. Pay special attention to the choice of words, especially the adjectives used.

Language help
honest · upright · corrupt · artificial · lively · sterile · planned · dangerous · colonial · challenging · inspiring · down-to-earth · powerful · enchanting · lulling · thriving · prosperous · gargantuan · humming · linear · sophisticated

3 Explain what Chief Sandayo means by the two final sentences. Make sure to contrast Lagos and Abuja based on your knowledge about the cities from 'Hope' (**A2**) and 'Home'.

Language help

while Abuja is …, Lagos is rather … • whereas … • compared to … • similar to … • different from … • in comparison to … • although … might be … • still better/worse than … • when contrasting … to … • when juxtaposing … with … • on the one hand …, on the other … • neither … nor … • despite …

Beyond the text

4 Writing Speaking Back in Lagos, Chief Sandayo meets his longtime friend Edosio Okafor, who also knows Abuja from personal experience. Edosio does not really understand why Sandayo has come back. Write their dialogue or carry out a role play in which Sandayo justifies his decision.

A4 Lagos beyond fiction

The following text gives you an insight into how Lagosians cope with the daily challenges of this city.

City of optimists *Robert Draper*

A recent survey of middle-class Nigerians conducted by […] an investment bank found that 76 percent of them are optimistic about the country's future. Sunniness of outlook has deep roots in Nigeria, particularly so in Lagos, a land of traders and settlers, and thus of
5 industrious disposition. Lagosians believe themselves to be pluckier than the average West African. This is, if anything, a modest self-assessment. […]

'If you give a Nigerian an opportunity, he will do his best,' a 36-year-old man named Onyekachi Chiagozie proclaimed one hot
10 afternoon as he proudly showed me his mobile electrician's workshop. In truth, the hollowed-out van with the cracked windshield wasn't much to look at. Chiagozie had bought the used van for about $4,300, and with it he could drive his tools all over the city, an enabler and beneficiary of Lagos's construction boom.
15 All of this was an improbable outcome for a young man who, at 18, became an unpaid apprentice to an electrician and worked odd jobs to survive. For a time he slept in a bus stop. He owned what he was wearing and nothing else. After about four years Chiagozie scraped together enough money to rent a tiny house in the mixed-income neighborhood
20 of Ojota, where he had apprenticed. 'Save, save, save: I've made the

The Lekki-Ikoyi link bridge, Lagos

5 industrious: busy, hard-working
5 disposition: (fml) character
5 plucky: courageous, brave
13 enabler: person who makes sth. possible
14 beneficiary [ˌbenɪˈfɪʃəri]: person who profits from sth.
16 apprentice: person who learns a business or craft from a master
16 odd job: small job, often involving repairing or cleaning things

sacrifice, and it's started to pay off,' he recalled. 'I registered my company. People in the area knew me. I'd fix this socket or see why that light wasn't turning on. The customers grew to trust me. Then they started getting me good jobs. Wiring whole houses. Fixing ATMs
25 and air conditioners. And because in Lagos it's very expensive to have an office, I decided to have the first mobile workshop in the country.'

The owner of the whimsically named Varied Pace Enterprises, Chiagozie beamed as he told me that he was now married, with a three bedroom house in Ojota and a tract of land outside the city that
30 he deemed a prudent investment. He shepherded me through the neighborhood, pointing out the houses that he and his two apprentices were currently wiring. The slum child had broken through. Another Lagos success story – but an unfinished one, for this was not nearly enough. 'I've been making money,' the electrician told me, 'but money
35 is better across the bridge, on the island. And I don't know the right people there yet.'

Banke Mechida Lawal knows the right people. When I visited her at her beauty salon, BM Pro, on Lagos Island, the young makeup artist was applying a full makeover to a wealthy client who would soon
40 be attending a wedding in Chicago. Because Lawal herself could not break away from her business to fly over for the event, a colleague was videotaping the procedure, and a copy would be sent to one of Lawal's beauty reps in the United States, who would replicate the makeover on the wedding day. Lawal's onetime fee was more than what it had cost
45 Chiagozie to buy his mobile electrician's workshop.

The makeup artist shares with the electrician a fierce entrepreneurial motor, though she began with a leg up on the ladder. Lawal's father was a university lecturer, her mother a radiologist. While studying English at the University of Lagos, she began doing other students' makeup
50 for a small fee. 'There was nothing like makeup artistry back then – it was unheard of,' she told me. 'But when I was traveling to the U.K. on holiday, I'd buy all sorts of makeup, and I was addicted to the girlie teenage magazines like *Marie Claire* and *Cosmo*. My background was in fine arts, and that helped me to put together colors and draw lines.'
55 During her post collegiate year of youth service mandated by the Nigerian government, Lawal decided to open a little cubicle in the affluent neighborhood of Ikoyi. In 2000 she did the makeup for the women in the wedding of the new president's son. Press coverage followed.
60 She moved to a larger studio. More celebrities requested her services, which now included hair and nails. Today BM Pro has four branches and 32 employees. Banke Meshida Lawal has what Onyekachi Chiagozie wants. She occupies the
65 dead center of island prosperity.

An aerial view of the Lekki-Ikoyi link bridge

22 socket: electrical outlet in a wall
24 wire sth.: equip e.g. a house with electrical wires
24 ATM = automated teller machine: machine from which you can get cash
27 whimsical: funny, light-hearted
28 beam: smile broadly
30 prudent: careful, sensible
43 rep = representative: (here) person who travels around a particular area offering a company's services
46 fierce: wild, passionate
46 entrepreneurial [ˌɒntrəprəˈnɜːriəl]: connected with running a business, especially your own business
50 fee: money paid for a service
55 mandate sth. [ˈ_ _] (esp. AE): make sth. obligatory for sb.
56 affluent: wealthy

'I know that what I do is ostentatious. It's luxury,' Lawal told me. 'Anyone can get by doing their own makeup themselves. But if they want that something special – make it go *pow*, give it that extra thing – they come to me. This is a cash economy, and there are people here 70 willing to pay cash.'

Smiling somewhat ruefully, the makeup artist added, 'The gap is so great between rich and poor. I'm glad to be on the receiving end of the cash.'

From: 'How Lagos has become Africa's boom town', in: National Geographic, January 2015

66 ostentatious [ˌɒstenˈteɪʃəs]: pompous, grandiose

Comprehension

1 Choose the correct answer(s). Prove you are right by indicating a line number.

a An optimistic outlook on Nigeria's future is held by …

> **A** the majority of the population.
> **B** 76% of Nigerians.
> **C** roughly three quarters of Nigerians from middle income groups.

(cf. l. _____)

b Compared to other Nigerians, Lagosians …

> **A** are more cheerful.
> **B** take chances more readily.
> **C** are more modest.

(cf. l. _____)

c Onyekachie Chiagozie says that if you want to make it in Lagos, you need to …

> **A** re-invest your earnings into business.
> **B** start a small business.
> **C** win the trust of customers.

(cf. l. _____)

d This way he has made a breakthrough and believes that …

> **A** he has made the most of his chances.
> **B** he ought to be content with that.
> **C** there still is potential.

(cf. l. _____)

e On Lagos island …

    A Lawal earns more with one makeover than Chiagozie does annually.
    B one makeover costs more than Chiagozie's electrician's workshop did.
    C Lawal's annual income is hardly more than Chiagozie's.

(cf. l. _____)

f Lawal and Chiagozie have a similar …

    A background.
    B spirit concerning business.
    C business strategy.

(cf. l. _____)

g The success of Lawal's business is a result of …

    A her customers in Chicago.
    B her talent.
    C its location on Lagos Island.

(cf. l. _____)

2 Compare Chiagozie's and Lawal's biographies by preparing a sequence diagram for each of them.

Analysis
3 Use your diagrams from task **2** to point out the essential elements that have contributed to Chigozie's and Lawal's success.

Beyond the text
4 Comment on the statement in l. 8 against the background of Chigozie's and Lawal's biographies.
5 Assess how close to reality the extracts from the novel in **A2** and **A3** are. Use the text by Robert Draper as a guideline.
6 `Writing` `Speaking` Imagine Chigozie, Lawal, Chike, Ifeoma and Chief Sandayo sitting together in a bar in Obalende market. Write a dialogue or prepare and carry out a role play in which each of them expresses their personal impressions, hopes and fears about living in this city.

Part B
Voices of Nigerian Women

B1 Role models in the family

Most people have role models, i. e. people who they try to imitate.

1 Collect ideas about role models in your family. Who are they? What makes them inspiring? What did they do for you? Make a word cluster.

Aunty Ifeoma *Chimamanda Ngozi Adichie*

Kambili is 15 and the daughter of a deeply Christian family living in Enugu. Shortly before Christmas, Kambili's aunt Ifeoma, a lecturer at the University in Nsukka, visits.

Aunty Ifeoma came the next day, in the evening, when the orange trees started to cast long, wavy shadows across the water fountain in the front yard. Her laughter floated upstairs into the living room, where I sat reading. I had not heard it in two years, but I would know that
5 cackling, hearty sound anywhere. Aunty Ifeoma was as tall as Papa, with a well-proportioned body. She walked fast, like one who knew just where she was going and what she was going to do there. And she spoke the way she walked, as if to get as many words out her mouth as she could in the shortest time.
10 'Welcome Aunty, *nno*,' I said, rising to hug her.
She did not give me the usual brief side hug. She clasped me in her arms and held me tightly against the softness of her body. The wide lapels of her blue A-line dress smelled of lavender.
'Kambili, *kedu*?' A wide smile stretched her dark-complected face,
15 revealing a gap between her front teeth.
'I'm fine, Aunty.'
'You have grown so much. Look at you, look at you.' She reached out and pulled my left breast. 'Look at how fast these are growing!'
I looked away and inhaled deeply so that I would not start to stutter.
20 I did not know how to handle that kind of playfulness. [...]
'*Nwunye m*,' Aunty Ifeoma called, and Mama turned back.
The first time I heard Aunty Ifeoma call Mama '*nwunye m*,' years ago, I was aghast that a woman called another woman 'my wife.' When I asked, Papa said it was the remnants of ungodly traditions, the idea
25 that it was the family and not the man alone that married a wife, and later Mama whispered, although we were alone in my room, 'I am her wife, too, because I am your father's wife. It shows that she accepts me.'
'*Nwunye m*, come and sit down. You look tired. Are you well?' Aunty Ifeoma asked.

05 cackle (n): sound comparable to the sounds chicken make
05 hearty: loud and cheerful
10 nno (Igbo): Welcome!
14 kedu (Igbo): How are you?
14 dark-complected: dark skinned
23 aghast: be shocked when hearing sth.
24 remnant: last remaining part of sth.

30 A tight smile appeared on Mama's face. 'I am well, very well. I have been helping the wives of our *umunna* with the cooking.'

'Come and sit down,' Aunty Ifeoma said again. 'Come and sit down and rest. The wives of our *umunna* can look for the salt themselves and find it. After all, they are here to take from you, to wrap meat in

35 banana leaves when nobody is looking and then sneak it home.' Aunty Ifeoma laughed.

Mama sat down next to me. 'Eugene is arranging for extra chairs to be put outside, especially on Christmas day. So many people have come already.'

40 'You know our people have no other work at Christmas than to go from house to house,' Aunty Ifeoma said. 'But you can't stay here serving them all day. We should take the children to Abagana for the Aro festival tomorrow, to look at the *mmuo*.'

'Eugene will not let the children go to a heathen festival,' Mama said.

45 'Heathen festival, *kwa*? Everybody goes to Aro to look at the *mmuo*.'

'I know, but you know Eugene.'

Aunty Ifeoma shook her head slowly. 'I will tell him we are going for a drive, so we can all spend time together, especially the children.'

Mama fiddled with her fingers and said nothing for a while. Then she

50 asked, 'When will you take the children to their father's hometown?'

'Perhaps today, although I don't have the strength for Ifediora's family right now. They eat more and more shit every year. The people in his *umunna* said he left the money somewhere and I have been hiding it. Last Christmas, one of the women from their compound even

55 told me I had killed him. I wanted to stuff sand in her mouth. Then I thought that I should sit her down, eh, and explain that you do not kill a husband you love, that you do not orchestrate a car accident in which a trailer rams into your husband's car, but again, why waste my time? They all have the brains of guinea fowls.' Aunty Ifeoma made

60 a loud hissing sound. 'I don't know how much longer I will take my children there.'

Mama clucked in sympathy. 'People do not always talk with sense. But it is good that the children go, especially the boys. They need to know their father's homestead and the members of their father's *umunna*.'

65 'I honestly do not know how Ifediora came from an *umunna* like that.'

I watched their lips move as they spoke; Mama's bare lips were pale compared to Aunty Ifeoma's, covered in a shiny bronze lipstick

'*Umunna* will always say hurtful things,' Mama said. 'Did our own

70 *umunna* not tell Eugene to take another wife because a man of his stature cannot have just two children? If people like you had not been on my side then …'

'Stop it, stop being grateful. If Eugene had done that, he would have been the loser, not you.'

---

30 tight: (here) with her lips pressed together
31 umunna (Igbo): clan
35 sneak sth. home: secretly take sth. home
43 mmuo (Igbo): masquerade
44 heathen: *heidnisch*
45 kwa (Igbo): sure
49 fiddle with sth.: handle sth. nervously
64 homestead: home and land surrounding it that is owned by a family

75 'So you say. A woman with children and no husband, what is that?'

'Me.'

Mama shook her head. 'You have come again, Ifeoma. You know what I mean. How can a woman live like that?' Mama's eyes had grown round, taking up more space on her face.

80 '*Nwunye m*, sometimes life begins when marriage ends.'

'You and your university talk. Is this what you tell your students?' Mama was smiling.

'Seriously, yes. But they marry earlier and earlier these days. What is the use of a degree, they ask me, when we cannot find a job 85 after graduation?'

'At least somebody will take care of them when they marry.'

'I don't know who will take care of whom. Six girls in my first-year seminar class are married, their husbands visit in Mercedes and Lexus cars every weekend, their husbands buy them stereos and textbooks 90 and refrigerators, and when they graduate, the husbands own them and their degrees. Don't you see?'

Mama shook her head. 'University talk again. A husband crowns a woman's life, Ifeoma. It is what they want.'

'It is what they think they want. But how can I blame them? Look 95 what this military tyrant is doing to our country.' […]

'*Ifukwa*, people are leaving the country. Philippa left two months ago. You remember Philippa?'

'She came back with you for Christmas a few years ago. Dark and plump?'

100 'Yes, she is now teaching in America. She shares a crammed office with another adjunct professor, but she says at least teachers are paid there.' Aunty Ifeoma stopped and reached out to brush something off Mama's blouse. I watched every movement she made; I could not tear my eyes away. It was the fearlessness about her, about the way she 105 gestured as she spoke, the way she smiled to show that wide gap.

From: Purple Hibiscus*, 2003*

84 degree: qualification you get after completing a university course

92 crown sth.: do an action which is the high point of a life and makes it complete

95 military tyrant: reference to some unnamed president

96 ifukwa (Igbo): *you see*

Comprehension

2 The excerpt reveals different attitudes towards Nigerian culture. Copy the table below and write what the people in the right-hand columns think of the situations **A–C**.

A Going to the Aro festival (cf. ll. 42–45)	Kambili's father: …	Everybody else: …
B Taking the children to the father's homestead (cf. ll. 49–64)	Kambili's mother: …	Aunt Ifeoma: …
C Getting married (cf. ll. 75–95)	Kambili's mother: …	Aunt Ifeoma: …

Analysis

3 a Describe your first impression of Aunt Ifeoma in no more than four sentences.

  b Prepare a character description of Aunt Ifeoma by completing the table below. Indicate whether direct or indirect characterization is used (cf. p. 24).

Impression	Evidence from text	Characterization direct indirect
	– cf. ll. 3–5	
A _____	– cf. l. 14	
B _____	– cf. l. 5	
C good-looking, striking	– cf. ll. 12–13	
	– cf. l. 16	
D agile, nimble	– cf. l. 6	
E _____	– cf. ll. 6–7	
F _____	– cf. ll. 7–8	
G spiteful, disrespectful	– cf. l. 52	
	– cf. l. 59	
H aggressive	– cf. l. 55	
I loyal	– cf. ll. 71–72	
J western, free-thinking, independent, educated	– cf. ll. 80–81	
K _____	– cf. l. 104	

  c Writing Write a characterization of Aunt Ifeoma.

4 a Illustrate the different roles of women in Nigerian society as they
are presented in the text

b Contrast Aunt Ifeoma's attitudes toward these roles with her sister-
in-law's and point out how Ifeoma's character matches her attitudes.

Beyond the text

5 Writing The conversation between Kambili's mother and Aunt
Ifeoma has made a lasting impression on Kambili (cf. her statement
in ll. 103–105). Work on task **a** or **b**.

a Write a dialogue in which Kambili talks to her older brother Jaja
about that impression.

b Write Kambili's diary entry in which she reflects about that impression.

6 Writing Imagine what role Ifeoma might play in Kambili's later life
and how this might also affect her relationship to her mother. Write
an entry to Kambili's blog that she writes at the age of 25 and in
which she reflects on who she is and on who influenced her. Consider
your results from **1** and **3b**.

B2 Women's reality through women's eyes

Comprehension

1 Listening Listen to the podcast in which Nigerian film director Tope   ◉ → **Track 01**
Oshin discusses with other women from 'Nollywood', i.e. the Nigerian
film industry. Look at the box below, then tick four issues which you
find central to their discussion.

○ gender equality	○ male dominance
○ women's social life	○ women's opportunities
○ female careers	○ female self-image
○ male and female attitudes	○ female role models
○ Nigerian culture	○ social realities
○ women's perspectives	○ Nigerian cinema

2 Summarize the podcast focusing on the four issues you have chosen.

3 Listen to the podcast again and write short answers or tick the
correct sentence ending.

a **Mildred Okwo** points out why women are better storytellers than
men. Name three aspects she mentions.

A _____

B _____

C _____

b In her daily work Mildred Okwo often has to deal with ...

    A governmental interference.
    B unstable weather conditions.
    C peoply trying to disturb the shoot.

c Amaka Igwe has been very influential because she ...

    A was known as a director not only in Nollywood.
    B was the only well-known African film director.
    C refused to work for the television industry.

d Amaka Igwe's way of thinking differed from Tope Oshin's in some respects. Write down three differences. Amaka Igwe believed that ...

    A _____

    B _____

    C _____

e Amaka Igwe's work has been an inspiration to women because she ...

    A built huge film studios in the east.
    B made women believe they could be film-makers.
    C successfully faced challenges in life.

f When **Nse Ikpe Etim** was cast for the movie *Journey to Self* she ...

    A didn't really believe in the female director.
    B was faced with her own prejudices about women.
    C was angry about the director being late.

g The realization that she was going to work with a female director struck Nse as ...

    A challenging.
    B unusual.
    C interesting.

h Name three social issues Tope Osin openly addresses in her movie.

A _____

B _____

C _____

i The film was not well received because …

    A it was released at the end of Tope Osin's career.
    B it was addressed to the average Nigerian audience.
    C it starred female protagonists.

j The 'culture of silence' means that women …

    A won't admit being victims of domestic violence.
    B play domestic violence down.
    C believe there is nothing wrong with domestic violence.

k In 2016 Nigerian Parliament turned down a bill for gender equality because it …

    A was considered incompatible with Nigerian culture.
    B granted women equal opportunities at work.
    C did not cover relevant aspects such as salaries and basic rights to life.

Analysis

4 Considering what you have found out in the podcast, evaluate how accurate the portrait of Nigerian women in 'Aunty Ifeoma' (pp. 41–43) is. Pay special attention to ll. 69–93. Give reasons for your opinion.

Beyond the text

5 `Writing` Write an article for a school magazine about the importance of female role models for teenage girls and young women. Explain why it might be important for them to have real as well as fictional role models. Contrast Nigerian and German perspectives.

6 Create a mind map in which you collect information about women's rights and their role in Nigerian society. Use categories such as domestic, social/cultural, professional, …

Part C
Voices of people's souls

C1 A Nigerian poet on his country

Comprehension

1 Read the poem below, then work on tasks **a** and **b**
to work out its meaning.

   a In the spaces provided below, rephrase each stanza in your own
words. The first stanza has been done and the second begun for you.

I sing of change *Niyi Osundare*	
I sing	*I sing about how beautiful Athens is without its slaves.*
of the beauty of Athens	
without its slaves	
Of a world free	*a world where there are no royals and no …*
5 of kings and queens	
and other remnants	
of an arbitrary past	
Of earth	
with no	
10 sharp north	
or deep south	
without blind curtains	
or iron walls	
of the end	
15 of warlords and armouries	
and prisons of hate and fear	
Of deserts treeing	
and fruiting	
after the quickening rains	
20 Of the sun	
radiating ignorance	
and stars informing	
nights of unknowing	
I sing of a world reshaped	
From: Niyi Osundare, I Sing of Change*, 1981*	

6 remnants (pl): part of sth. that is left over   **7** arbitrary: not based on reason, often considered unfair   **15** warlord: leader of an unofficial military group fighting against other groups within a country   **15** armoury: building in which people who are not professional soldiers are trained   **21** radiate sth.: send sth. out in all directions

b In your own words, sum up what kind of world the speaker is
dreaming of.

Analysis

2 a From the statements below choose the one that, in your opinion,
expresses the poem's central idea best.

> The poem's central idea is a world …
>   **A** without injustice, social hierarchy or war.
>   **B** in which everything has to be remade.
>   **C** which changes and finally achieves justice.
>   **D** where people learn from the past to make a better future.

b Discuss your choice with a partner.

3 Especially in poetry, images are often used to illustrate ideas.

a Match the images from the poem (in the table on the left) with
a suitable interpretation (on the right). Write the correct
combination of letter and number in the column on the right.

Image	Interpretation	
A 'the beauty of Athens without its slaves' (l. 2f.)	**1** a world in which no group is dominating another group simply because they were born into this position	_____
B 'a world free of kings and queens' (l. 4f.)	**2** the blissful state of not knowing too much, of not worrying about things	_____
C 'earth with no sharp north or deep south' (ll. 8–10)	**3** a place where nobody is living on the edge of society or being exploited	_____
D 'warlords and armouries' (l. 15)	**4** a world of plenty, of growth, of powerful nature	_____
E 'deserts treeing and fruiting' (l. 17f.)	**5** a world which is not divided, e.g. along the lines of wealth	_____
F 'the sun radiating ignorance' (l. 20f.)	**6** wars and violence	_____

Quotes from: Niyi Osundare, 'I sing of change', 1981

b There are four more images in the poem. Identify them and
interpret them yourself.

4 The tone of a text expresses the writer's attitude toward its subject
matter. From the box below choose the adjective which in your
opinion defines the poem's tone best (→ Info box on p. 30). Explain
your choice.

Language help
solemn · playful · serious · concerned · ironic · hopeful · visionary · sarcastic ·
humorous · thoughtful · provocative · persuasive · inspirational · polemic · satiric · …

5 Reconsider your results from tasks **1–4**, then from the options below
choose the one that comes closest to your interpretation of the
poem. You may also write your own interpretation.

'I sing of change' …
    A … is about the potential that lies in the world and in its people.
    B … expresses a hope that despite the challenges facing the world, everything will
        change for the better.
    C … expresses the belief that in spite of seemingly insurmountable problems it is
        still important to speak out for a better future.
    D … is about a person who believes in and works for a better future for his country.

My own interpretation: _____

_____

_____

Beyond the text
6 Being a Nigerian writer, Osundare may be expressing some criticism
of Nigeria in his poem. Outline what Nigerian problems he might be
referring to.
7 Writing Think of problems and challenges you see in your world.
Write your own 'I sing of change' poem portraying your ideal world.

C2 A Nigerian poet on his people

Read the following poem by Ben Okri, one of the foremost African writers.
(The questions on the right refer to task **2**.)

African elegy *Ben Okri*

We are the miracles that God made
To taste the bitter fruit of Time.
We are precious.
And one day our suffering

5   Will turn into the wonders of the earth.

What is the speaker talking about?

There are things that burn me now
Which turn golden when I am happy.
Do you see the mystery of our pain?
That we bear poverty

10   And are able to sing and dream sweet things

Who is addressed? What is 'the mystery of our pain'?

And that we never curse the air when it is warm
Or the fruit when it tastes so good
Or the lights that bounce gently on the waters?
We bless things even in our pain.

15   We bless them in silence.

That is why our music is so sweet.
It makes the air remember.
There are secret miracles at work
That only Time will bring forth.

What are the effects of this mysterious pain?

20   I too have heard the dead singing.

What do the dead tell the speaker in their song?

And they tell me that
This life is good
They tell me to live it gently
With fire, and always with hope.

25   There is wonder here

And there is surprise
In everything the unseen moves.
The ocean is full of songs.
The sky is not an enemy.

Where does the speaker see surprise?

What might the ocean stand for?
What might the sky stand for?

30   Destiny is our friend.

From: Ben Okri, An African Elegy, *1992*

title elegy [ˈelədʒi]: song or poem expressing sadness or sorrow   **3** precious: important, valuable
9 bear sth.: carry sth. heavy   **11** curse sb./sth.: talk badly about sb./sth.   **13** bounce: jump
14 bless sb./sth.: (here) talk positively about sb./sth.   **19** bring forth sth.: reveal sth., make sth. visible
27 the unseen: (here) God

Comprehension

1 Summarize each stanza of the poem in one or two sentences.
2 Answer the questions given next to the poem.

Analysis

3 Explain how the poem's content in stanzas 1–3 differs from that in stanzas 4–6. Then point out the poem's subject matter.
4 Copy the table below.
   a Find examples of the stylistic devices in the poem and write their lines in the middle column.
   b In the right-hand column, write what effect or meaning they might have.

Stylistic device	Example from the poem (lines)	Effect or meaning
Enjambement (i.e. incomplete syntax at the end of the line where the meaning runs over to the next line without any punctuation at the end)	…	…
Parallelism (i.e. the deliberate repetition of similar or identical words, phrases, sentence constructions, etc. in the same or a neighbouring sentence)	…	…
Imagery (i.e. figurative language. Images are meant to stimulate the reader's/listener's imagination and give them a new perspective on a particular topic or idea. Examples: metaphor, personification, simile, symbol)	…	…
Diction (i.e. the words a writer chooses for their text. Diction is very important as words influence the reader/listener; cf. the use of words with a positive/negative connotation, emotive language.)	…	…

5 Describe the poem's tone and interpret its message.

Beyond the text

6 Look at ll. 21–24 again.
   a With a partner, discuss whether this piece of advice might also be relevant for young people living in Germany.
   b <mark>Writing</mark> Write an article for a youth magazine in which you discuss how a positive outlook on life is important for young people.

Part D
Voices from Nigeria's unquiet north and nouth

D1 On the run *Helon Habila*

One of the challenges Nigeria is facing is the terror carried out by Boko Haram, a jihadist terrorist organization that is active especially in northeastern Nigeria. Its mission is to rid Nigeria of Western influences and to impose the Shariah, i. e. Islamic law. Originally formed as a non-violent group, Boko Haram is today considered one of the deadliest terror groups, launching attacks on the police, the military and civilians.

In his book *The Chibok Girls*, Nigerian writer Helon Habila describes raids on Nigerian villages carried out by Boko Haram. In the extract below, eyewitness Mallam Kyari recounts what happened to his family.

'That was their third coming. They came around 3:47 p. m., I remember the exact time because we had just finished praying in the mosque. At the time, my father, the Chief Imam, Allah bless his memory, was still alive. My father went on home, and I remained behind. The noise of
5 their shooting was everywhere. And I thought to myself, these people are here, and when they take over a town, they just don't leave immediately. They stay for months, even years. In Gwoza they were there for about nine months. They even killed the emir of Gwoza.

'And we decided we couldn't stay. We must leave. At home I found
10 my wife, who told me the children had gone to the well to fetch water. I told her, "You, start running toward Mife. I will go toward the well and gather the children." I went on my motorbike. But before going I went into the main house and told my parents we had to run, these people are killers and we can't wait for them to find us here. We all set out and
15 I went on my bike to the well, but no one was there. The children weren't there. Only shoes and jerry cans and buckets strewn all over the place.

'And just then I saw their car coming. It was a pickup, and if they had wanted to kill us then, they could have. They were driving through very fast, and their target was the military camp. That was what saved
20 us; they could surely have killed us.

'That night, we slept near a village called Kubumbula. We slept in an open farm, there must have been about a hundred persons with us. In the morning some were saying, surely they must have left by now. But others said, no, let's wait. If they are gone, word will soon get to us. By
25 7:00 a. m., they started shooting again. We could hear them. I was thinking about my wife and my children. I hadn't seen them since I left home.

8 emir (Arabic): governor
16 jerry can: container used to transport liquids

'I decided to go look for them. First I had to get fuel for my bike. I headed for Kubumbula, following the burtali [cow trail]. In Kubumbula I met my brothers and sisters, so many people, but no one had seen my
30 wife and children. I went on to Mife – there I met my wife, but not the children. We were told they were in another village, Gaglan. I took my wife on the bike and we went on to Gaglan.

'On the way, I met an elder, a good friend of my father's. The first thing he told me was, "Have you heard about your father?" I said, "No."
35 He said, "Well, your father fell while running. His blood pressure rose and he collapsed." He said my younger brother had gone to Gaglan to look for me. So, I went into Gaglan and met my brother, Bana, there. He told me our father fell, just after Chibok, before Gaglan. […]

'The only thing it is okay to kill are animals, and only for food. If you
40 are not going to eat it, don't kill it. How then can you kill a man, who is just like you, with hands and feet and life just like yours, who has done nothing to you, you never knew him or met him before, how can you question his existence, and even kill him? […] They now even kill other Muslims, they throw bombs in mosques while people are praying.
45 Islam doesn't sanction that. This is just a sect with its own doctrine and its own way of thinking, but it is not Islam.'

From: Helon Habila, The Chibok Girls*, 2017*

33 elder: (here) older person with authority
45 sanction sth.: approve of sth., authorize sth.

Comprehension

1 Fill in the table to give a structured account of the incidents mentioned by Kyari.

Place	People involved	Incidents, news
mosque	*father*	
Kyari's home		*no children*
well	–	
way to Kubumbula	–	
barn near Kubumbula		
Kubumbula		
Mife		
way to Gaglan		
Gaglan		

Analysis

2 Kyari talks about a number of incidents that must have left him with strong feelings such as fear of death; yet he seems fairly unemotional. Examine how this impression is created. Consider syntax, stylistic devices and choice of words.

Beyond the text

3 The Boko Haram assaults need to be seen against the backdrop of religious conflicts in northern Nigeria that reach back into the early 19th century.

   a Do some research about religious conflicts in northern Nigeria, covering their emergence in the 19th century and developments in the 20th and 21st century. The names, places and events in the box below can help you in your research.

> Mohammed Yusuf · The People Commited to the Propagation of the Prophets's Teachings and Jihad · Yelwa Massacres · Boko Haram Insurgency · Abubakar Shekau · Abuja Headquarters Bombing · Borno State · President Goodluck Jonathan · Chibok · Idrissa Timta · #BringBackOurGirls · …

   b Draw a timeline presenting your results. Compare results with a partner.

4 **Writing** Write a news story about the incidents presented in 'On the run', about the conflicts that form its background and their consequences for the population. The words below must be used in the given order.

> migration · refugee(s) · refugee camps · religious tensions · suffering · orphan(s) · widow(s) · challenge · government · radicalism · radicalization · continuance · misunderstanding · peace · bloodshed · divide · bordering states · insecurity · Abuja · Lagos · hope · security · future · solutions

5 Look at ll. 43–46 again ('They … praying'). Discuss what Kyari's words might mean for the coexistence of Muslims and Christians in northern Nigeria and the reputation of Islam in Nigeria.

D2 Life in paradise? *Helon Habila*

You are going to read an excerpt from Helon Habila's *Oil on Water*. The novel is set in the Niger Delta, the centre of Nigeria's crude oil production.

1 a Before reading the excerpt, describe the photograph in detail.
  b Point out what associations the photograph evokes for you.
  c Find a suitable title.

In this excerpt from *Oil on Water*, the chief of a village in the Niger Delta tells the story of his community.

Once upon a time they lived in paradise, he said, in a small village close to Yellow Island. They lacked for nothing, fishing and hunting and farming and watching their children growing before them, happy. The village was close-knit, made up of cousins and uncles and aunts and
5 brothers and sisters, and, though they were happily insulated from the rest of the world by their creeks and rivers and forests, they were not totally unaware of the changes going on all around them: the gas flares that lit up neighbouring villages all day and all night, and the cars and TVs and video players in the front rooms of their neighbours who had
10 allowed the flares to be set up. Some of the neighbours were even bragging that the oil companies had offered to send their kids to Europe and America to become engineers, so that one day they could return and work as oil executives in Port Harcourt. For the first time the close, unified community was divided – for how could they not be tempted,
15 with the flare in the next village burning over them every night, its flame long and coiled like a snake, whispering, winking, hissing? Already the oil-company men had started visiting, accompanied by important politicians from Port Harcourt, holding long conferences with Chief Malabo, the head chief, who was also Chief Ibiram's uncle.
20   One day, early in the morning, Chief Malabo called the whole village to a meeting. Of course he had heard the murmurs from the young people, and the suspicious whispers from the old people, all wondering what it was he had been discussing with the oil men and the politicians.

5 insulated from sth.: separated from sth.
6 creek: very small river
7 gas flare: flame used to burn surplus gas in order to keep it from igniting accidentally
11 brag: show off, talk about sth. you have in a self-satisfied way
13 executive: person working in a high position in a company
14 tempt sb.: make sb. do sth. by offering them sth.
16 wink at sb.: close and open an eye quickly
16 hiss: make a long, continued 's'-sound
22 suspicious: having the feeling that sb. has done sth. wrong without having any proof

Well, they had made an offer, they had offered to buy the whole village,
25 and with the money – and yes, there was a lot of money, more money
than any of them had ever imagined – and with the money they could
relocate elsewhere and live a rich life. But chief Malabo had said no, on
behalf of the whole village he had said no. This was their ancestral land,
this was where their fathers and fathers' fathers were buried. They'd
30 been born here, they'd grown up here, they were happy here, and
though they may not be rich, the land had been good to them, they
never lacked for anything. What kind of custodians of the land would
they be if they sold it off? And just look at the other villages that had
taken the oil money: already the cars had broken down, and the cheap
35 television and DVD players were all gone, and where was the rest of
the money? Thrown away in Port Harcourt bar rooms, or on second
wives and funeral parties, and now they were worse off than before.
Their rivers were already polluted and useless for fishing, and the land
grew only gas flares and pipelines. But the snake, the snake in the garden
40 wouldn't rest, it kept on hissing and the apple only grew larger and
more alluring each day. And already far off in the surrounding waters
the oil-company boats were patrolling, sometimes openly sending
their men to the village to take samples of soil and water. The village
decided to keep them away by sending out their own patrols over the
45 surrounding rivers, in canoes, all armed with bows and arrows and clubs
and a few guns. But daily Chief Malabo was feeling the pressure. As a
chief he had no control over the families' decision about what to do
with their land, but as a chief his word carried weight, especially among
the elders. But what of the young men who were still grumbling, and
50 looking enviously across the water at the other villages?

From: Helon Habila, Oil on Water, *2011*

27 relocate: move to somewhere else
27 on behalf of sb.: in sb.'s name
28 ancestral [æn'sestrəl]: handed to the people by earlier generations
32 custodian: person who protects and takes care of sth.
41 alluring: attractive and exciting
43 soil: ground
45 club: stick with one end thicker than the other, used as a weapon
50 envious: wanting to have what sb. else has

Comprehension

2 Point out the village's development by making a sequence diagram
(→ Info box). Follow these steps:
– Divide the development into separate sequences.
– Make notes about each of them on large Post-it stickers using your
own words.
– Add influences from outside the village to the diagram.
– Present your sequence diagram to a partner and discuss it with
him/her.

Info **A sequence diagram**

Starting point → Step 1 → Step 2 → Step ... → Goal/final point

3 Describe how the villagers change under the influence of the oil industry.

Analysis

4 a Complete the grid below to analyse the author's choice of words and use of imagery. Also consider the connotation of words and possible allusions, e. g. to religious concepts.

Word / image / phrase	General meaning	Interpretation
'Once upon a time' (l. 1)	*traditional beginning of a fairy tale*	*reference to a time when life was perfect*
'paradise' (l. 1)	*religious concept: …*	*situation in the village before …*
'tempted' (l. 14)		
'flare' (l. 15)		
'coiled like a snake' (l. 16)		
'winking, hissing' (l. 16)		
'suspicious whispers' (l. 22)		
'the land only grew gas flares and pipelines' (l. 38)		
'the snake in the garden wouldn't rest' (l. 39)		
'the apple only grew larger' (l. 40)		
…		

Quotes from: Helon Habila, Oil on Water, *2011; cf. p. 56f.*

b Write a coherent text analysing how the author emphasizes the village's development through his use of stylistic devices.

Beyond the text

5 Speaking Imagine the elders, who follow Chief Malabo's guidance, and the young villagers, who want a more modern life, hold a discussion. Work in two groups.
  a One group collects arguments for the older villagers' position, the other group for the younger villagers' position. Think of ways of countering the other group's arguments (cf. task **2**).
  b Hold the discussion.

Chapter IV

Nigeria's Young Voices and Dreams

Part A
Musicians and film-makers speaking up

A1 'Mrs Nollywood': Mo Abudu

Nigeria is home to the second largest film industry worldwide, which is often referred to as Nollywood. The following audio file portrays one of its most influential makers, Mo Abudu.

Comprehension

1 [Listening] Listen to the radio report and tick the correct sentence ending(s) on p. 60. Sometimes more than one answer is correct.

◎ → **Track 02**

Annotations:
- CEO = chief executive officer: Geschäftsführer/in
- household name: well-known name
- Hillary Clinton (born 1947): American politician and writer, First Lady of the USA (1993–2001), nominee for US president in 2016
- 'Moments with Mo': daily talk show on African TV hosted by Mo Abudu

a Mo Abudu …

    A became CEO of EbonyLife TV in 2015.
    B was named the world's most successful woman in media in 2015.
    C founded EbonyLife TV in 2015.
    D has produced a lot of Nigerian blockbusters.

b EbonyLife TV is a media network which …

    A has become very popular beyond Africa.
    B was launched a few decades ago.
    C focuses on local broadcasting.
    D aired a show called 'The First Lady of Chat'.

c Mo Abudu …

    A has been in the media business since her university days.
    B defines herself as a creative entrepreneur.
    C was kicked out of her managing career.
    D regrets having started her TV career in her 40s.

d According to Mo Abudu, Africa's image in the world …

    A is based on prejudice.
    B is restricted to famine and poverty.
    C is formed by the image presented in the media.
    D needs changing by transnational TV programmes.

Beyond the text

2 Mo Abudu mentions four ideas that people associate with Africa. Write them down.

3 The starting point of Mo Abudu's career as a film producer was her realization that Africa's negative image needed to be changed.

  a Conduct a survey among your friends, family, fellow students etc. to find out what idea of Africa prevails.

  b `Speaking` Analyse your results and make a graph or chart representing them. Present your graph or chart to the class.

  c Present your graph or chart to the class, comparing your results to Mo Abudu's (cf. task **2**).

4 `Speaking` Do some research on Mo Abudu's films and present your results to class.

Mo Abudu

A2 The West and perceptions of Africa

In an interview with the BBC in 2015, Mo Abudu talked about her
ideas on how Western media influence the perception of Africa.   ⊙ → **Track 03**

1 Viewing Watch part of the interview (→ Annotations) and outline
Mo Abudu's view on …

a the role of Western media in shaping Westerners' views on Africa.

_____

_____

b the influence of Western media within Africa.

_____

_____

c how this situation can be changed.

_____

_____

d her role as a female African media producer.

_____

_____

Annotations:
- Oprah Winfrey (born 1954): US-American talk show host and television producer,
  best known for 'The Oprah Winfrey Show', a talk show that aired between 1986
  and 2011
- 'Moments with Mo': daily talk show on African TV hosted by Mo Abudu
- Mugabe = Robert Mugabe (born 1924): Zimbabwean Prime Minister (1980–1987)
  and President (1987–2017), who has been accused of being a dictator, of crimes
  against humanity and human rights abuses
- EbonyLife television: African black entertainment network launched by Mo Abudu

Beyond the text

2 Writing Mo Abudu thinks it's important to empower African women.
Do some research on the role of women in Africa and remember what
you found out in **Chapter 3**, **Part B**, then write a comment on Mo
Abudu's view.

A3 An interview with Efe Oraka *Nii Ak*

Nigeria is a nation of manifold young and creative voices. The following is an interview with Efe Oraka, a Nigerian music artist.

1 Before reading the interview reflect on what music means to you. Make notes.

Who's Efe ? What is music to you?

Efe is a 17-year old girl who simply loves music. Music to me is a different art of its own. It not only contains the sonic aspect, but there's also a spiritual aspect to it. It's something that can never be exhausted or that can age. Something that transcends the complexities of this
5 world and goes to a whole other dimension. It's not really something that can be put in a box or contained. Neither is it something that can be fully understood. It is poetry and sound and passion and light all wrapped up in perfect balance. Really, music is life. The absence and presence of it make such a profound difference in the world. Far more
10 than what we can conceive. Music is life.

'Music is life', that's quite profound.
How can you relate this to your life, being a young African girl pursuing the art of music?

For me music has always been a means of self-expression and escapism.
15 As a 'young African girl' in my little African corner, each day I am constantly thrown ideals on who I should be, how I should dream, what I should look like, how I should sound etc. The world around me constantly tells me what it feels I ought to be doing with my life. Getting a law degree so I can 'shine-eye' for my in-laws, being domesticated
20 and learning how to be a 'proper African woman'. Although these are all good, they aren't all expedient to my sole purpose in life. And unfortunately, I am not a very vocal person when it comes to speaking my mind, and standing up for myself, that's where the struggle sets in. But you see, music has always provided me a voice to say the things
25 that are unheard of. It reminds me that I don't have to sound like anyone else or be like anyone else and that I'm just fine as myself. I've struggled in the past trying to combine who everyone wants me to be and who I should be. I was reaching to find an equilibrium. But now that I have a better understanding (although not a full understanding) of music,
30 I can confidently create the art I feel I should create.

Creating music with such profound ideologies, how do you own this passion and craft the art?

These ideologies, these concepts on what music means to me were not just conceived in a day. They were gotten from years of pondering and
35 questioning different things. The understanding of music that I have has helped me hone my craft and sharpen my sword in that I now understand who my music is. My music is a subset of myself. […]

2 sonic: connected to sound
3 exhaust sth.: (here) use sth. up
4 transcend sth.: go beyond sth.
10 conceive sth.: (here) imagine sth.
14 escapism: outlook on life which ignores all negative aspects
19 shine-eye (v, infml): make a friendly face
19 in-law (n): person you are related to by marriage
19 domesticated: (here) limited to the sphere of the household
21 be expedient to sth.: contribute to sth.
22 vocal (adj): (here) telling your opinion with confidence
28 equilibrium: balance
32 craft sth.: make sth. using special skills
34 ponder: think about sth.
36 hone sth.: (here) develop sth.
36 craft (n): work
37 subset: part

What's the balance of making music the world can see as a global set in Africa, expressing values of an African woman and still being
40 understandable to every woman?

Is there really a balance? Because you see, putting out art you feel is consistent and congruent with all the aforementioned categories is quite subjective. Some female artists make music they feel can be accepted globally, portray the details of an African woman and be relatable with
45 women all over, but really is their music perceived by the public as that? It's a matter of context. I feel that being an African woman, I have some experiences, both positive and negative, that my other African sisters can share with me, but women from other parts of the world cannot relate to. The same way some general struggles of 'being a woman' are
50 not at all that general. For instance, I was speaking about rape to a friend who lives abroad and her views were completely different to my grandmother's views. So I don't really think all the categories can be reconciled. Really, I just make music that comes out of my experiences and I hope people, not just women, can relate to it and appreciate it
55 because it would be quite a struggle trying to combine everything and make it acceptable for everyone. After all, art is more about expression than it is about acceptance.

Being a young mind born in the new age shaping a new identity for Africa, how does your music uphold both, morals of your mind
60 **and the culture?**

The new age is all about pushing down boundaries that were set by our predecessors, challenging our minds to create things that really portray who we are and not who we are told to be. The morals of my mind and the ones of the culture (to me) are quite easily intertwined so it's not
65 difficult to put them together. I don't really try to create anything to specifically conform to the culture (really). I guess it just happens. I'm all for mental emancipation, creativity and diversity. To me, this is what the culture upholds so it's really not a struggle to find a balance. Although like I said earlier, there is no balance. I'm just creating.
70 **What's the new age culture to you and your art?**

To me the new age culture is all about embracing oneself. Showing forth what makes you unique as a person, being creative, being an active member of society and advancing in innovations and such. It's about breaking boundaries and saying *no* to limits. It's also about pushing
75 oneself and your immediate society to help raise awareness of the imminent change. It's creativity and togetherness as a bond. Not being afraid to stand for what you believe in and being the very best you can be. [...]

Can music be a change to help shift the culture of Africa, especially
80 **the ones built on the ethos of new age Africa?**

Yes, music can. From what I've seen from a lot of artists, there is a high level of genre bending. People are really pushing things, you know?

42 be congruent with sth. ['kɒŋgruənt]: match sth., be in line with sth.
44 be relatable with sb.: (here) able to be connected to sb.
53 reconcile sth.: (here) harmonize sth.
59 uphold sth.: (here) stick to sth. you believe to be right
62 predecessor ['priːdəsesə]: sb. who held a specific position before us
64 intertwined: (here) closely connected
76 imminent: about to happen very soon
80 ethos ['iːθɒs]: set of ideas, spirit
82 genre bending: (here) mixing of different kinds of music

You listen to a song that you think is reggae at first but somehow it's Afro beat and pop as well! It's amazing. It can change the culture in the
85 way that the culture can become more flexible. Music has no race so I wouldn't use the word *anglicized*, but rather a lot of the sounds coming from Africa will have a far-reaching impact because they suit the African ear but also suit the Caucasian, European, Asian and so on. The music is really showing how much thought and heart new age artists
90 put into their craft. It's a revolution and it's amazing.

From: the website of narroweddown.wordpress.com, *26 January 2017*

86 anglicized: adapted to the English culture
88 Caucasian (n): person with pale skin

Comprehension
2 Outline Efe's understanding of music and her self-conception as a young Nigerian woman.

Analysis
3 Compare Efe's understanding of music to yours.
4 Examine Efe's use of language to get her ideas across. Consider style and tone (→ Info box below and on p. 30)

> **Info Style**
> Style is the way in which a text is written. In order to examine the style of a text it is necessary to examine aspects such as the register (i.e. formal/informal language), the diction and the tone of the text (cf. p. 30), as well as the grammar and syntax used.

Beyond the text
5 `Writing` Write an email to Efe in which you respond to her ideas on music and identity.

A4 Young musicians calling for change

The following radio report from 2017 (→ Annotation) introduces you to some Nigerians talking about how music can bring about change in Nigeria.

Annotation:
settlement: official compromise that ends an argument between two parties involved

Audio online:
cornelsen.de
Code: navubi

Comprehension
1 `Listening` Listen to the radio report and tick the correct sentence ending(s). Sometimes more than one answer is correct.
   a In the past Ogoniland has been shaped by …

   A its geographical position in the Niger Delta.
   B large scale oil exploitation.
   C massive environmental pollution.
   D its lively music scene.

b MC Kay became a musician because …

    A it had been his dream as a fisherman.
    B he needed money for his family.
    C he sees it as a form of political participation.
    D his dad, who died early, had wanted him to go into music.

c The settlement with Royal Dutch Shell in 2015 …

    A was fought for at court in the Netherlands.
    B motivated MC Kay to write his song 'January Money'.
    C provided sufficient financial compensation.
    D changed the image of the oil company.

d Village Chief Eric Dooh …

    A made 'January Money' widely known in Ogoniland.
    B criticizes young artists like MC Kay.
    C sees the young musicians' potential in shaping the region's future.
    D would not waste the compensation money on building a music studio.

e Reggae singer Tumsi …

    A says that Ogoniland has been let down by politics.
    B feels that many young people have the will to change their future.
    C complains about the lack of infrastructure in the region.
    D strongly believes that God will bring change to Ogoniland.

f The journalist Alloy Khenom …

    A says that the lack of possibilities makes young people turn to crime.
    B urges the government to offer people opportunities and support.
    C organizes concerts with Nigerian music stars from Lagos.
    D sees music as a key to overcoming profound problems.

Beyond the text

2 Writing Speaking The men talking in the radio report are convinced of the power of music to bring about change in their country. Do you believe that music can have such power? Give a two-minute speech or write a comment, giving examples to support your view.

Part B
Nigerian dream(s)

B1 Nigerian dream *Efe Oraka*

In A3, you read an interview with the musician Efe Oraka. Here's her song on the Nigerian dream.

Before reading
1 You have certainly come across the concept of the American dream.
   a With a partner, briefly exchange ideas on what the American dream means.
   b Speculate on what the Nigerian dream might imply.

We've got a house in Maitama
Buy three more on Banana Island
Been working hard since forever
So we can finally ask;
5 'Do you know who I am?'
Daddy don't come home on business trips
He's busy with the Lagos 'big girls'
Living it up
And mama makes these appearances
10 Don't want no one to notice the bruises and cuts …

We're so sad
But we're living the Nigerian dream
We've been had
But we look so happy or so it seems
15 With hypocritical smiles
Fake fake laughs
We've reached the all time low …
We're so sad
But we're living the Nigerian Dream …

1 Maitama: exclusive area in Nigeria's capital Abuja
2 Banana Island: artificial island in the Lagos lagoon and the most exclusive place in Nigeria
8 live it up: sich austoben
10 bruise: injury
13 have been had: have been tricked
15 hypocritical: not real
16 fake: not real

20 Go home for the holidays
Gotta show everyone we've made it
We are so stuck in our ways
Don't even know the difference between love and hatred
Oh but the kids are messed up … so messed up
25 Let's just pretend that they're not stressed
'Cause "Nigerians don't get depressed"
Gotta keep the appearance up
'Hush! The neighbors might hear us' …

We're so sad
30 But we're living the Nigerian dream
We've been had
But we look so happy or so it seems
With hypocritical smiles
Fake fake laughs
35 We've reached the all time low …
We're so sad
But we're living the Nigerian Dream …

Don't we look so happy with our fake smiles?
Don't we look so pretty in the lies we've told?
40 Pretending everything is alright
But inside we're cold

Don't we look so happy with our fake smiles?
Don't we look so pretty in the lies we've told?
Pretending everything is alright
45 But inside we're cold …

From this Nigerian Dream, I hope we wake up …

© 2018 Efe Oraka

Comprehension
2 Sum up what the speaker complains about.

Analysis
3 Analyse how the song's message is conveyed. Focus on use of
language and stylistic devices.

Beyond the text
4 With a partner, collect instances of hypocritical behaviour that you
have witnessed, then work on either **a** or **b**.
 a Speaking Prepare and give a speech addressed to the
 hypocritical person.
 b Writing Add one or two verses on hypocrisy to Efe Oraka's song.

B2 What exactly is the Nigerian dream? *Ayomide O. Tayo*

The article gives a disillusioned account of the Nigerian dream.

The Nigerian dream is a reflection of a society where justice does not prevail and where corruption is tolerated.
Have you ever asked yourself what the Nigerian dream is?
A lot of people believe that the Nigerian dream is to travel and settle
5 abroad. While we have witnessed a steady and mass movement of people from here to overseas since the 80s, this isn't the Nigerian dream.

Yes, many Nigerian youths dream of getting away from here and settling in greener pastures abroad. This, however, isn't a dream. We cannot ignore the reality that many Nigerians find themselves abroad –
10 doing menial jobs and living from paycheck to paycheck.

Not every Nigerian who travels abroad to settle is guaranteed a life of comfort and stability. Many learn quickly that life on the other side is not a bed of roses that Hollywood sold to them. There are plenty of Nigerians who want to come back home but they can't because they
15 are ashamed that they will be coming back with nothing.

This is not the Nigerian dream because many are living in nightmares abroad. So, what is the Nigerian dream? It is simple. The dream is to make it by any means necessary.

Think about it for a second. Life in Nigeria is 'solitary, poor, nasty,
20 brutish, and short.' The life expectancy here is 53 years of age. 67% of Nigerians live below the poverty line. The constant supply of electricity is still a myth. Police brutality is high with operatives of the Special Anti-Robbery Squad extorting, illegally detaining and assaulting Nigerian youths daily. Inside this heap of harsh conditions called Naija
25 lies the Nigerian dream, a perverted ambition. The Nigerian dream is simply this: 'to succeed against all odds, by any means necessary'. And there are a lot of odds. Apart from the aforementioned ones, add a non-existent public health care system, poor level of education and unemployment. The odds are stacked against the Nigerian youth to
30 make it in life.

Nigerians are tenacious, they will succeed despite the obstacles. With our backs against the wall, we have continuously found a way not only to survive but to thrive as well.

Let me break down the word 'succeed' in this context into street lingo
35 you are familiar with. Succeed here means 'hammer', or 'blow'. When a Nigerian says 'I wan blow', that is just the Nigerian dream. When Olu Maintain sang 'When I hammer, first thing na Hummer' on 'Yahooze', that is just the Nigerian dream in play.

Our country people just don't want to get by. They want to be
40 successful, they want to have lots of money because tomorrow is not guaranteed. In a society where there aren't strong safety nets (reliable pension scheme and good health care) people will enter the rat race.

2 prevail: exist
8 pasture: land covered with grass where you keep e.g. cows
10 menial job: badly paid job that doesn't need specific qualifications
19 nasty: unpleasant
20 brutish: violent, unkind
23 extort sb.: get sth. from sb. through threats
23 detain sb.: keep sb. in an official place and not let them go
23 assault sb.: attack sb. violently
24 Naija: (here) Nigeria
26 odds: probability
29 stack sth.: put things onto each other in a neat way
31 tenacious: determined, not giving up easily
34 lingo (infml): language
35 hammer: hit sth. hard
35 blow: hit something forcefully

The aim will be to be able to make the most amount of money within the shortest possible time.

45　That is why as Nigerians we do not operate on a long-term level. Your landlord asks you for a year's rent upfront despite knowing you get paid monthly. He wants the rent for a year because who knows, by tomorrow you could get fired with no notice or your company starts to owe you months of salary.

50　The American dream is to have a nice house with a picket fence, the identity of middle-class America. In Nigeria, the middle class is very thin, one wrong move you are in poverty land.

'Any means necessary' means we are willing to bend the rules (also break the rules) to be rich. The high level of corruption indicates how 55　we are willing to break the rules to make it in life in a society that has lost its moral compass.

In a society where there is little or no justice and safety nets, citizens would do all within their means to have a decent life. And this is what is happening in Nigeria right now. From politicians to every day 60　Nigerians, we are trying to grab as much cash within the smallest amount of time to ensure we have a fulfilling life.

This is why we have Internet fraudsters. The dream to 'hammer' and 'blow' is what fuels crime in this country. Young men are willing to do anything it takes to be rich in a society where the odds are stacked 65　against them.

Perhaps we shouldn't call it the Nigerian dream but rather the Nigerian nightmare. If life is hellish here then surely the dreams you have cannot be beautiful but rather a perversion of healthy ambition.

And this is why the Nigerian society is excessively materialistic. The 70　drive to show you are better than your neighbour comes from the crabs in a barrel mentality. You want to flaunt because you want to announce that you have made it from the hellhole. You want to proudly proclaim that you did all that it took to be successful.

This is the Nigerian dream, the burning desire to be successful against 75　all odds by any means necessary. Take a look around and you will see that most of the successful people believe in this dream.

From: the website of pulse.ng*, 6 June 2018*

46 upfront: paid in advance
48 notice: the advance time period when sb. should be informed about the ending of a contract, e.g. an apartment rental contract
53 bend the rules: change the rules so as to suit your interests
70 crabs in a barrel mentality: mentality based on the belief that if you cannot have sth., then nobody else should have it
71 flaunt: present yourself in a certain way to impress people

A nice house with a picket fence

Comprehension
1 Outline the problems Nigerians have to face and the concept of the Nigerian dream as presented in the article.

Analysis
2 Analyse how Tayo presents the concept of Nigerian dream. Focus on line of argument and stylistic devices used.

Beyond the text
3 In small groups discuss Tayo's statement about the American Dream in l. 50.

B3 **The end of a dream?** *Bernadette Mittermeier*

1 **Mediating** Work on either **a** or **b**.
  a You have been invited to take part in the Youth Forum on Migration, which is aimed at sharing young perspectives on migration from all over the world. Write a speech presenting reasons why Nigerians may try to leave their country.
  b An English friend of yours who doesn't understand much German has read the introduction to the article and wonders why Abiazie has not been able to find 'Sicherheit' in Germany. Write her an mail answering her question.
  c In your politics class you are dealing with measures to help make Nigeria a safer place. Give a short presentation on national and international measures that have been taken and on their success.

Info Mediation

When mediating from one language to another, the first step is to analyse the communicative situation: who are you talking to or writing for? What aspects of the topic will they need to know or be interested in? What kind of text will you be producing – is it a blog post, a speech in front of your class, a chat among friends , …? Once you're aware of the situation, start identifying the pieces of information that are relevant for your task. Don't worry if your mediated text appears very short – this is normal because you select only the information you need.
After you've collected the necessary information, structure it and start producing your text. Consider …
  – aspects that are specific to a culture and need explaining
  – the text type you are dealing with
  – the appropriate style and register
  – whether you will speak or write – when speaking, you can use non-verbal means of communication
  – how to phrase words that you don't know in the other language: make sure you know how to paraphrase.

Die Wahlen bieten für Nigerianer keine Hoffnung. Viele sind schon vor langer Zeit nach Deutschland geflohen. So wie Ifeanyi Abiazie. Doch auch hier fand er keine Sicherheit.

Am schlimmsten ist die Stille, sagt Abiazie. Wenn es still ist, fängt er an
5 nachzudenken. Über das, was er „den Vorfall" nennt. Über die drei Tage in einer stickigen Gefängniszelle, über seine Familie in Nigeria, und über den Gerichtstermin, von dem er nicht weiß, wann dieser kommt und ob Abiazie danach in Deutschland bleiben darf. Wenn er von den zwei Jahren seit seiner Flucht erzählt, ist seine Stimme monoton und so leise,
10 dass man ihn mit dem Radio im Hintergrund kaum versteht. Seine leicht milchigen Augen schauen aus dem Fenster, nicht zu seinem Gegenüber.

Ifeanyi Abiazie ist ein großer Mann, 35 Jahre alt, jemand, der viel vor-hatte mit seinem Leben. Jetzt sitzt er in einem bayerischen Café und sieht zu, wie sein Kaffee kalt wird. Sein Leben in Deutschland besteht
15 aus Stille und Warten.

Viele Nigerianer kommen nach Deutschland, auf der Suche nach einem besseren Leben oder einfach nur nach Sicherheit. Sie sind die viertgrößte Gruppe der Geflüchteten hier, nach Syrern, Irakern und Iranern. Die meisten von ihnen haben keine Chance, Asyl zu bekommen.
20 Die Schutzquote schwankt um die 15 Prozent. Denn die deutschen Behörden gehen davon aus, dass die meisten Nigerianer innerhalb ihres Landes Schutz finden könnten.

Doch das Land kämpft mit einer ganzen Reihe von Konflikten, mit denen die Bundesregierung sich beschäftigen muss, wenn sie Flucht-
25 ursachen aufarbeiten will. Jedes dieser Probleme hat schon für sich das Potenzial, die staatlichen Strukturen einstürzen zu lassen. Vor den Präsidentschaftswahlen an diesem Samstag haben sich die Konflikte noch verschärft: Die Zahl der Terroranschläge und die Gewalt sind gestiegen. Deshalb fliehen so viele Nigerianer nach Europa.
30 Dem Bundesamt für Migration und Flüchtlinge (Bamf) wäre es trotz-dem lieber, wenn Ifeanyi Abiazie im Südwesten Nigerias geblieben wäre. Er sei in einem anderen Landesteil sicher. Doch im Süden kämpfen Rebellengruppen und Seperatisten gegen das nigerianische Militär. Und im Norden gilt neben dem weltlichen Recht das islamische, die Scharia.
35 Dort wäre Abiazie vielleicht gesteinigt worden – wegen des „Vorfalls".

Es passierte am Valentinstag 2016. Abiazie verbrachte ihn mit einem „männlichen Freund", wie er ihn nennt. In Nigeria ist Homosexualität strafbar. Das Land ist extrem konservativ, sogar Küsse zwischen Män-nern sind verboten. „Wenn du mit jemandem ausgehen willst, musst du
40 zahlen", erklärt Abiazie. Er kaufte seinem Date Jeans, Sneaker und ein Handy, erzählt er. Abends gingen sie in den Park, tranken und unter-hielten sich. Abiazie war gut gelaunt und wurde unvorsichtig. Er küsste seinen Freund.

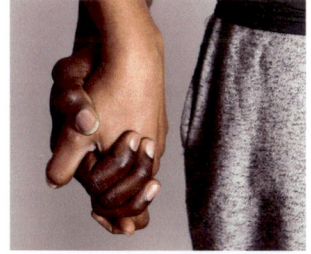

„Eine Gruppe Männer sah uns. Sie waren in einer Gang. Diese Mafiosi
45 trifft man in der Stadt öfter. Sie bedrohen dich mit ihren Pistolen, bis du ihnen alles gibst, was du bei dir hast", erzählt Abiazie. „Sie fingen an uns zu schlagen, wollten uns töten. Eine Polizeistreife rettete uns."

Aber die Polizisten nahmen nicht die Gangmitglieder mit. Sie ver-hafteten Abiazie und seine Begleitung. Den Polizisten erzählte der
50 „Freund", Abiazie habe ihn zu den Küssen gezwungen. Er kam frei, Abiazie blieb in der Zelle zurück. Auf Homosexualität stehen bis zu 14 Jahre Gefängnis.

„Die politischen Ämter dienen der Bereicherung der Herrschenden"
In den Norden kann Abiazie nicht nur deshalb nicht fliehen, weil er
55 schwul ist. Für christliche Geflüchtete wie ihn ist es dort besonders

71

gefährlich, denn im Norden attackiert Boko Haram noch immer Zivilis-
ten. 2014 galt die Gruppe als tödlichste Terrororganisation der Welt. Ein
Jahr später, im Dezember 2015, verkündete Präsident Muhammadu
Buhari: „Boko Haram ist technisch besiegt." Für eine Weile sah es so
60 aus, als sei das wahr.

Denn Boko Haram hatte sich zurückgezogen, an die Grenze zu Niger,
Tschad und Kamerun. Besiegt sind die Terroristen aber noch nicht. Seit
letztem Herbst steigt die Zahl der Toten und der Anschläge wieder, auch
das Militär greift die Gruppe wieder offen an. Präsident Buhari hatte zu
65 seinem Antritt versprochen, Boko Haram zu besiegen. Dass die Terroristen
jetzt wieder da sind, schadet seiner Wiederwahl-Kampagne.

Deshalb ist es wahrscheinlich, dass einige von Buharis politischen
Gegnern Boko Haram mit Geld unterstützen, erklärt der Politologe Jan
Sändig. Er forscht an der Universität Tübingen über die Terroristen.
70 „Einige Politiker versuchen, die Gruppe zu instrumentalisieren." Verurteilt
wurde noch niemand, Korruption ist allgegenwärtig: „Die politischen
Ämter dienen der Bereicherung der Herrschenden", sagt Sändig.

Auch Ifeanyi Abiazie setzt keine Hoffnung in die Wahlen: „Die Alten
kontrollieren alles und wollen die Jungen nicht mitmachen lassen.
75 Präsident Buhari ist 76 Jahre alt, im Rentenalter, jemand, der monate-
lang seine Arbeit nicht machen konnte, weil er krank war. So jemand
will das Land regieren. Für mich hat er nichts zu bieten."

Die Gang hatte seine Zeit im Gefängnis genutzt

Während die Eliten extrem reich sind, hungert der Großteil der
80 Bevölkerung. Fast die Hälfte der Nigerianer lebt von weniger als 1,90
Dollar am Tag, schätzt die Weltbank. Und das Problem wächst mit der
Bevölkerung: In den vergangenen 50 Jahren hat sie sich vervierfacht.
200 Millionen Einwohner hat Nigeria. Bis 2050 könnte es das Land mit
der drittgrößten Bevölkerung sein, nach Indien und China.
85 Abiazie merkte das früher in seinem Alltag, wenn er sich durch die
Menschenmassen auf den Straßen von Lagos drängen musste, der größten Stadt Nigerias. Hier hatte er sein Leben aufgebaut. „Ich denke nicht
darüber nach, was meine Regierung für mich tun kann. Ich frage mich,
was ich selbst für meine Zukunft tun kann", sagt Abiazie. Sein Mantra
90 klingt ein wenig wie eine nigerianische Version von Kennedys berühm-
ten Zitat, sein Optimismus erinnert an den Amerikanischen Traum: „Du
kannst alles erreichen, wenn du selbst daran arbeitest", glaubt Abiazie.

Er studierte Wirtschaft und baute einen Laden für Elektrogeräte auf,
mit Geld, das er sich von der Bank lieh. Nach fünf Jahren hatte er ein
95 laufendes Geschäft und fünf Mitarbeiter unter sich. „Mir ging es gut",
sagt er. Dann kam der Valentinstag.

Drei Tage saß Abiazie in der Zelle, erzählt er. Schließlich ließen
die Polizisten ihn laufen, für ein Bestechungsgeld von umgerechnet
1200 Euro. Als er zu seinem Laden kam, fand er ihn zerstört vor. Die

100 Gang hatte seine Abwesenheit genutzt, die Scheiben eingeschlagen und seine Waren gestohlen.

„Ich wusste nicht, wo ich hin sollte", erzählt Abiazie heute. „Mein Geschäft war ruiniert, ich hatte noch immer Schulden bei der Bank. Mein Anwalt sagte mir, dass die Polizei mich jederzeit wieder verhaften 105 und anklagen könnte." Abiazie wollte zu seiner Familie in den Osten fliehen. Doch die hatten bereits von dem Vorfall gehört und einen Brief des örtlichen Herrschers bekommen. In Nigeria gibt es noch eine Reihe von Monarchen, die zwar offiziell keine politische Macht mehr haben, regional aber trotzdem oft einflussreich sind. In dem Brief stand, dass 110 seine Familie Abiazie nicht aufnehmen durfte, sonst sei auch ihr Leben in Gefahr. Er versteckte sich bei einem Freund, für acht Monate. Nur nachts traute er sich auf die Straße. Abiazie musste weg. Aber wohin?

Fluchtursachen zu bekämpfen, wird schwierig

Eine Flucht ins Ausland ist für die meisten Nigerianer zu teuer. Etwa 115 zwei Millionen sind deshalb innerhalb des Landes auf der Flucht, schätzen die Vereinten Nationen. Doch in Nigeria überlagern sich die Konflikte: muslimischer Norden gegen christlichen Süden, Arm gegen Reich, Polizisten gegen Gangs, das Militär gegen Boko Haram, Seperatisten und andere Rebellengruppen, und auf dem Land gehen sess- 120 hafte Bauern und nomadische Hirten mit Macheten und Gewehren aufeinander los, weil sie sich um Weideflächen streiten – eine Auseinandersetzung, durch die schon mehr Menschen getötet wurden als durch die Terroristen. Wer hier Fluchtursachen bekämpfen möchte, der hat eine schwere Aufgabe vor sich.

125 Deutschland hat immer wieder betont, eben das versuchen zu wollen. Als die Kanzlerin im August 2018 Nigeria besuchte, waren die Erwartungen groß. Nigeria hofft auf eine engere Zusammenarbeit, Deutschland darauf, viele Geflüchtete problemlos zurückschicken zu können. Das Thema stand zwar nicht auf der offiziellen Tagesordnung. Angesprochen 130 wurde es doch. „Wir sind gegen illegale Migration", sagte Nigerias Präsident Buhari. Konkrete Pläne für eine Rückführung vereinbarten Merkel und Buhari aber nicht.

„Die deutsche Entwicklungszusammenarbeit mit Nigeria konzentriert sich auf die nachhaltige Wirtschaftsentwicklung", heißt es auf der 135 Seite des Bundesministeriums für wirtschaftliche Zusammenarbeit und Entwicklung. 57,6 Millionen Euro gab Deutschland dafür 2016 aus.

Das kann Deutschland tun

Der Politikwissenschaftler Sändig ist pessimistisch. „Um Nigeria zu helfen, müsste man bei ganz grundlegenden Dingen anfangen, wie dem 140 Aufbau stabiler staatlicher Strukturen", erklärt Sändig. „Das sind sehr langfristige Unterfangen."

Auch das Militär zu unterstützen ist heikel: „Selbst die USA sind davor zurückgeschreckt, Kampfhubschrauber zu schicken, weil dem

nigerianischen Militär so brutale Menschenrechtsverletzungen vorge
145 worfen werden", so Sändig. Gar nichts tun könne aber auch keine
Lösung sein. Die beste Chance böten kleine, lokale Entwicklungsprojekte.

Sichere neue Heimat? „Plötzlich brannte es."

Ifeanyi Abiazie schaffte es über einen Umweg nach Deutschland:
Eine katholische Gruppe wollte nach Italien, für eine Konferenz, und
150 konnte ihn mitnehmen.

Von Rom aus buchte er einen Zug nach München. Er lebt nun in einer
Unterkunft in Nußdorf am Ilm, einem kleinen Ort wenige Gehminuten
von der österreichischen Grenze entfernt. Im März wurden er und die
anderen Bewohner mitten in der Nacht geweckt. „Es war kurz vor
155 Mitternacht. Plötzlich brannte es", erinnert sich Abiazie. Zum Glück
wurde niemand verletzt. Das Feuer hätte sich schnell ausbreiten können, stellte ein Richter später fest. Die Polizei fand zwei mit Benzin
gefüllte Flaschen und ein Hakenkreuz an der Außenwand, das jemand
Tage zuvor mit schwarzer Farbe gesprüht hatte. Nur zwei Wochen später
160 gab es wieder einen Brandanschlag.

„Ich kann mir nicht erklären, wer uns angreifen wollte", erzählt
Abiazie. Was er nicht wusste: Die beiden Täter kehrten nach dem zwei-
ten Anschlag zurück, mit dem Einsatzwagen der Freiwilligen Feuerwehr,
um den Brand zu löschen, den sie selbst gelegt hatten. Die Polizei konnte
165 die beiden jungen Männer später festnehmen. Auf dem Computer des
einen fand die Polizei Nazi- und Hitlerbilder mit verharmlosenden
Texten. Sie wurden zu drei Jahren und neun Monaten Haft verurteilt.

Nach den Anschlägen konnte Abiazie noch weniger schlafen als davor. Er nahm Antidepressiva, doch die halfen kaum. Im Mai kam der
170 zweite Tiefpunkt: Das Bamf glaubt Abiazie nicht. Er sei in Nigeria sicher.
Gegen die Entscheidung könne er aber klagen. Also tat er das.

Das ist jetzt ein Jahr her. Seitdem wartet er. Auf den Gerichtstermin.
Darauf, dass seine Heimat Nigeria wieder zu einem Land wird, in dem
er sicher leben kann. Oder darauf, dass zumindest Deutschland zu seiner
175 neuen Heimat wird. „Ich verstehe, wenn Deutschland wenig für Nigeria
tun kann", sagt Abiazie. Aber sein Leben als Flüchtling hier ein wenig
sicherer machen, das könnte Deutschland schon, findet er.

From: 'Ein nigerianischer Traum scheitert', Süddeutsche Zeitung, *23 February 2019*

Partner B

Chapter I: Approaching the Giant of Africa

A2 Nigeria – facts and figures

1 Guess the relevant figures for **Nigeria** and fill them in the table below. The figures for Germany may help you as a reference.

	Nigeria	Germany	South Africa
Religions	_____ % Muslim _____ % Christian _____ % others _____ % none	55.3 % Christian 5 % Muslim 2.7 % others 37 % none	_____ % Muslim _____ % Christian _____ % traditional African _____ % others _____ % none
Land area	_____ km²	357,022 km²	_____ km²
Population	_____ (rank ____ in the world)	80,457,737 (rank 19 in the world)	_____ (rank ____ in the world)
Population below poverty line	_____ %	16.7 %	_____ %
Urban population	_____	77.3	_____
Literacy rate	_____ %	99 %	_____ %
Unemployment rate	_____ %	3.8 %	_____ %

Statistics from: www.cia.gov, 2019

2 Speaking Your partner will tell you some facts about **Nigeria**. If necessary, provide him/her with the right figures from the table below. Discuss which facts surprised you most.

	Nigeria	Germany	South Africa
Life expectancy	59.3 years	80.9 years	_____ years
Median age	18.3 years	47.4 years	_____ years
Access to improved drinking water supply	68,5 %	100 %	_____ %
Access to improved sanitation facilities	29 %	99.2 %	_____ %
Access to electricity	59.3 %	100 %	_____ %
Internet users	25.7 %	89.6 %	_____ %
GDP by sector Agriculture	21.1 %	0.7 %	_____ %
Industry	22.5 %	30.7 %	_____ %
Services	56.4 %	68.6 %	_____ %

Statistics from: www.cia.gov, 2019

Language help
have a life expectancy of … · have access to … ·
be provided with … · account for … % of the GDP

Annotations
- median age: The age from which point half of the population is younger and the other half is older
- GDP = gross domestic product: *Bruttoinlandsprodukt*

3 Speaking Present your findings for the table from task **1** to your partner and ask him/her for the correct figures. Correct your table if necessary. Discuss which facts surprised you most.

Language help
be affiliated with a religion · cover an area of … ·
the fourth most populous country in the world … · amount to sth.

Now go back to task **4** on p. 8.